MAJOR ISSUES IN
REGULATION

MAJOR ISSUES IN REGULATION

Regulation Lectures 1992

Sir Gordon Borrie · Sir James McKinnon

Sir Sydney Lipworth · Mr Alan Booker

Sir Bryan Carsberg · Dr David Fisk

Prof. S.C. Littlechild ·

The Rt. Hon. Christopher Chataway

Introduced and edited by Prof. M.E. Beesley

Institute of Economic Affairs
in association with the
London Business School
1993

First published in July 1993
by
THE INSTITUTE OF ECONOMIC AFFAIRS
2 Lord North Street, Westminster, London, SW1P 3LB

in association with the

London Business School

IEA Readings 40

ISSN 0305-814X
ISBN 0-255 36324-9

The Institute gratefully acknowledges financial support for its publications programme and other work from a generous benefaction by the late Alec and Beryl Warren.

Printed in Great Britain by
Bourne Press, Bournemouth, Dorset

Text set in Times Roman 11 on 12 point

CONTENTS

Major Issues in Regulation

Contents

INTRODUCTION

Professor M. E. Beesley
London Business School

THE SECOND SERIES of Regulation lectures, the papers given at which appear in this IEA Readings, was held at London Business School from March to June 1992. As in the first series, they arose from intense interest in the operations of competition law and the privatised utility acts, the principal strands of regulatory action in industry and commerce in the UK. This 1992 series was intended to provide those responsible for the conduct of regulation with a forum in which to discuss, with interested professionals, the important issues facing them.

They took the opportunity with enthusiasm, as the lectures reprinted here will show. They are useful, first of all, for their accessible, but definitive accounts of what the several regulatory tasks are. The utility acts are by no means uniform in the degrees of freedom allowed a regulator to influence company actions, or in his ability to acquire the knowledge he needs, or in the degree to which the Monopolies and Mergers Commission can determine, directly or indirectly, the outcomes of utility regulation. **Sir Sydney Lipworth's** exposition underscores this variation, leading him to speculate both about MMC's future role *vis-á-vis* the specialist regulators, and their future independence.

Sir Gordon Borrie addresses the questions of reform of competition policy as a whole, writing from his long experience in shaping it. The paper constitutes what is, in effect, his advice in the current Green Paper debate on future legislation in this area. His twin thrusts, for more effective enforcement, embracing private actions, and powers to investigate suspected abuse of monopoly power, will be regarded by many as highly likely to appear in that legislation.

Utility regulators have varying opportunities, depending on the constraints exerted by the economic facts of their industries and their Act, to increase competition by encouraging entry. Three of the contributions focus on this task, and show the differing ways in which the regulators approach it.

The central issue for **Sir James McKinnon** is establishing a means to develop acceptable ways for newcomers to contract for delivering their gas over a distribution network at arm's length from the incumbent gas trader, and in a totally transparent way. The difficulties he records in mounting an entry policy will be particularly interesting reading now that British Gas has been referred to the MMC.

Sir Bryan Carsberg, in one of his last papers before leaving Oftel to become Director General of Fair Trading, sees the problem as one of managing entry, including the setting of initially favourable interconnect terms as an inducement, how to make consistent the terms enjoyed by the variety of entrants to follow Mercury after the Duopoly Review, and maintaining price control on BT; and the question of when inducements are to stop.

Professor Stephen Littlechild, inheriting a structure in electricity more clearly differentiating monopoly from other elements, and one initially more favourable to competition, also inherited greater expectations about how fast competition would develop. He shows how the various elements having a bearing on his duty to promote competition are related - rules governing generators, RECs purchasing, pool rules and contracts for differences. A wide-ranging set of possibilities for reform is canvassed.

In the more unchallengeable utilities, water and airports, the concerns necessarily focus on the operation and development of price controls. Privatisation Acts and subsequent licences emphasised the prices to be charged, critical to flotation and companies' finances. Regulators have had most of the job of dealing with the collateral, non-price, elements. **Mr Alan**

Booker presents OFWAT's thinking on how quality dimensions can be developed, and set alongside a critique of charges, through using comparators between companies. Part of the regulators' armoury, in taking this forward, he argues, is to involve other industry interests - consumers, investors and management - in developing acceptable measures.

Mr Christopher Chataway's concern in price regulation centres on the relationship between price controls and investment. But his remit goes beyond BAA; his position is unique among the regulators in that he has responsibilities all through the chain of production from tour operations back through airlines, airports and even in the direct production of essential services to the industry. He shows the complexity and difficulty of his rôle, but is clear that, with all its warts, current utility regulation is superior to the régimes which went before it.

All the regulators represented in these lectures have individual styles, important to the firms they interact with. **Dr David Fisk** poses what is perhaps the most fascinating question of all - the ways in which regulation itself creates industrial innovation, thus changing both the competitive status of regulated firms and the task of regulation. He concludes that regulation inevitably creates differential advantages for some players, actual or potential. The utility regulators would, probably, agree with this judgement. But the question which follows - *quis custodiet ipsos custodes?* - though recognised, as in Sir Sydney Lipworth's paper, is one to which answers have yet to be found.

Six of our discussants were kind enough to provide written versions of their presentation. These are also included in the book.

The lectures and discussions can, I think, be said to have fulfilled the hopes expressed in the book of the 1991 series, that the reversal of rôles between academics and regulators in 1992 would provide a welcome opportunity to continue the dialogue between regulators and their knowledgeable critics. In 1993, the series continues under the IEA's sponsorship, putting academics into the spotlight again. We are fortunate indeed that the professional regulators will also, again, be taking the chairs on these evenings.

The views expressed in this *IEA Readings* are those of the authors, not of the Institute (which has no corporate view), its Trustees, Directors or Advisers.

THE AUTHORS

Michael Beesley is a founding Professor of Economics at the London Business School. Lecturer in Commerce at the University of Birmingham, then Reader in Economics at the LSE, he became the Department of Transport's Chief Economist for a spell in the 1960s. He has advised on company problems of monopoly and restrictive trade practices and on the relationships between nationalised industries and their Ministries. His work in the London Business School has centred on the implications for management in, and the management by the government of, organisations receiving public financial support, and the issues of deregulation and privatisation in telecoms, transport, water and electricity. He started the Small Business Unit at the School, a focus for entrepreneurship.

His widely known work in transport economics and telecoms policy has taken him to such countries as Australia, USA, India, Pakistan, Hong Kong, South Korea, Cyprus and many in Europe. His independent economic study of *Liberalisation of the Use of British Telecommunications' Network* was published in April 1981 by HMSO and he has since been very active as an advisor to the Government in telecoms, the deregulation of buses and the privatisation of the water industry. For the IEA, of which he is a Managing Trustee, he wrote (with Bruce Laidlaw) *The Future of Telecommunications* (Research Monograph 42, 1989) and (with S.C. Littlechild) 'The Regulation of Privatised Monopolies in the United Kingdom', in *Regulators and the Market* (IEA Readings No.35, 1991).

He has been a Visiting Professor at the Universities of Pennsylvania (1959-60), British Columbia (1968), Harvard Business School and Economics Department (1974), McQuarie, Sydney (1979-80). He was appointed CBE in the Birthday Honours List, 1985; and he became

Director of the PhD programme in the same year. In 1988 he became a member of the Monopolies and Mergers Commission.

Alan Booker joined OFWAT in November 1990 as Deputy Director General of Water Services. He was formerly Managing Director of Biwater Supply Limited and of Bournemouth & West Hampshire Water Companies, and Chief Executive of East Worcestershire Water Company.

Alan Booker is a Civil Engineer by profession and a Fellow of the Institution of Water and Environmental Management. He was educated at Dronfield Grammar School near Sheffield and trained as a Mining Engineer with the National Coal Board before graduating from the University of Sheffield with a First-Class Honours degree in Mining Engineering in 1960.

He worked in Sheffield, Birmingham and South Wales in the water supply industry until 1974 when he became Operations Manager for Welsh Water responsible for water, sewage and river management in South Wales. In 1980 Mr Booker became Managing Director of the East Worcestershire Water Company where he remained until 1988, when he took part in a management buy-out of the company in association with Biwater. Alan Booker now lives in Droitwich, Worcestershire, and is married with three children.

Sir Gordon Borrie, QC, was Director of Fair Trading from 1976 to 1992. He received his knighthood in the 1982 Queen's Birthday Honours List and was appointed a Queen's Counsel in 1986.

Born in 1931, Sir Gordon was educated at the John Bright Grammar School, Llandudno, and then at the University of Manchester where he graduated LLB (Hons.) in 1950 and LLM in 1952. The University awarded him an honorary LLD in 1990. He was a Harmsworth Scholar at the Middle Temple and called to the Bar in 1952. (He was elected a Master of the Bench of the Middle Temple in 1980.) He did his National Service with British Commonwealth Forces, Korea, 1952-54.

After practice at the Bar in London, he moved to the University of Birmingham where he was Professor of English Law, 1969-76, the Dean of the Faculty of Law, 1974-76. He was a member of the Council of the Consumers' Association, 1972-75, and also served on a number of government bodies, including the Parole Board for England and Wales and the Consumer Protection Advisory Committee.

Sir Gordon became President of the Institute of Trading Standards Administration in 1992 and later in the same year Chairman of the Commission on Social Justice, set up by the Leader of the opposition. He is also currently Chairman of the Money Advice Trust and a Director of the Woolwich Building Society, Mirror Group Newspapers and Three Valleys Water Services.

He is the author or part-author of a number of publications dealing with legal and consumer matters, including *Commercial Law* (6th edition, 1988), *The Consumer, Society and the Law* (with Professor A.L. Diamond, 4th edition, 1981), and *Law of Contempt* (with N.V. Lowe, 2nd edition, 1983). For the IEA he contributed a paper, 'Reflections on Regulation', to *Regulators and the Market* (IEA Readings No.35, 1991).

Sir Bryan Carsberg has been Director General of the Office of Fair Trading (OFT) since June 1992. He was previously Director General of the Office of Telecommunications (OFTEL) from 1984 to June 1992. He qualified as a Chartered Accountant in 1960. After four years in private practice, he became a lecturer in accounting at the London School of Economics and Political Science (LSE) and a visiting lecturer at the University of Chicago. He gained an MSc (Econ.) at the London School of Economics in 1967. In 1969 he was appointed Professor of Accounting and Head of the Department of Accounting and Business Finance, University of Manchester, and later Dean of its Faculty of Economic and Social Studies. From 1978 to 1981 he was Assistant Director of Research and Technical Activities and Academic Fellow with the Financial Accounting Standards Boards, USA. In 1981 he became Arthur Andersen Professor of Accounting at the LSE and part-time Director of Research for the ICA. He is the author of numerous accountancy publications and has also undertaken various consultancy assignments in accounting and financial economics. For the IEA he contributed a paper, 'Competition and the Duopoly Review', to *Regulators and the Market* (IEA Readings No.35, 1991). He was awarded his knighthood in January 1989.

The Rt. Hon. Christopher John Chataway's career has been divided between the public and private sectors. After reading PPE at Magdalen College, Oxford, and four years with ITN and the BBC, he was a Member of Parliament for North Lewisham (1959-66) and Chichester (1969-74). He was a junior Education Minister in the Macmillan Government (1962-64) and Minister in the Heath Administration (Minister of Posts and Telecommunications, 1970-72; Minister for Industrial Development, DTI, 1972-74; appointed PC in 1970). From 1974 he was for 15 years Managing Director of Orion Royal Bank. He has been a non-executive Chairman or Director of a number of companies since 1974. He became Chairman of the Civil Aviation Authority in June 1991.

Dr David John Fisk is Chief Scientist of the DOE, and Director, Air Climate and Toxic Substances. His responsibilities include policy on climate change (where he leads the UK delegation to the International Negotiating Committee on a Framework Convention on Climate Change), on air pollution, and on toxic substances and the deliberate release of genetically modified organisms. As Chief Scientist he is responsible for the development of DOE science policy.

After studying Natural Sciences at Cambridge (MA) and Low Temperature Physics at Manchester (PhD), he joined the Department of the Environment (Building Research Establishment) in 1972 to research the modelling of the propagation of road traffic noise. In 1974 he took charge of work concerned with energy conservation economics and work on energy efficiency of heating systems. In 1979 he became head of BRE Mechanical Engineering Division, responsible for research in lighting and building services. He has published 40 papers on building science, systems theory and economics. In 1983 he was awarded the degree of Doctor of Science by the University of Cambridge for work on systems and control theory.

In 1984 he became Assistant Secretary, Department of the Environment, responsible for Environmental Policy Planning. He led UK delegations to North Sea Conference, and Acid Rain negotiations in the European Community.

Dr Fisk is Visiting Professor, School of Architecture, University of Liverpool; he is a Chartered Engineer, and a Fellow of the Chartered Institute of Building Services.

Sir Sydney Lipworth, QC, was Chairman of the Monopolies and Mergers Commission (MMC) from 1988 until April 1993; he had previously been a part-time member from 1981. He was educated at the University of the Witwatersrand, Johannesburg (BCom, LLB), was admitted as a solicitor in 1955 and called to the South African Bar in 1956. He practised as a barrister in Johannesburg, 1956-64. He was a founder and Deputy Chairman of Allied Dunbar Assurance and a director of other public companies. He has written on investment, taxation, life insurance and pensions. Sir Sydney was knighted in January 1991.

Stephen Littlechild was appointed the first Director General of Electricity Supply on 1 September 1989. He has been Professor of Commerce, University of Birmingham, since 1975. He was formerly Professor of Applied Economics, University of Aston, 1973-75, and sometime Consultant to the Ministry of Transport, Treasury, World Bank, Electricity Council, American Telephone & Telegraph Co., and Department of Energy.

He is author or co-author of *Operational Research for Managers* (1977), *Elements of Telecommunication Economics* (1979), and *Energy Strategies for the UK* (1982). For the IEA he wrote *The Fallacy of the Mixed Economy* (Hobart Paper 80, 1978, Second edn. 1986), and contributed to *The Taming of Government* (IEA Readings No.21, 1979), *Agenda for Social Democracy* (Hobart Paperback 15, 1983), and *Regulators and the Market* (IEA Readings No.35, 1991). He has been a Member of the IEA Advisory Council since 1982. He was commissioned by the Department of Industry to consider proposals to regulate the profitability of British Telecom. His Reports, *Regulation of British Telecommunications' Profitability*, and *Economic Regulation of Privatised Water Authorities*, were published in 1983 and 1986 respectively.

Sir James McKinnon was appointed the first Director General of Gas Supply on 24 June 1986. The term of appointment has been extended to 1994. He has over 30 years' experience of international business in general and financial management. Recently he has been consulted on the development of the gas supply business in Eastern Europe. The unique developments in the UK gas market have created a high level of interest in various parts of the world.

Sir James is a member of the Institute of Chartered Accountants of Scotland and was its President in 1985-86. He is also a member of the Institute of Cost and Management Accountants. He has written several publications, including a series of books on Management Accounting for the Institute of Cost and Management Accountants' examination students. For the IEA he contributed a paper, 'Regulation of the Gas Sector', to *Regulators and the Market* (IEA Readings No.35, 1991). He was knighted in 1991.

HOW CAN UK COMPETITION POLICY BE IMPROVED?

Sir Gordon Borrie
Director General, Office of Fair Trading

ANYONE EXAMINING the UK's competition legislation for the first time must be struck first of all by its complexity. Since the first statute of 1948 which set up the Monopolies Commission, the legislation has evolved piecemeal so that we now have four basic statutes, the Fair Trading Act 1971, the Restrictive Trade Practices Act 1976, the Resale Prices Act 1976 and the Competition Act 1980, dealing with the control of mergers, anti-competitive practices and other forms of monopolistic behaviour, cartels and resale price maintenance. Each of these are dealt with by somewhat different procedures involving some mix of the four different authorities that are involved, the Director General of Fair Trading (DGFT), the Monopolies and Mergers Commission (MMC), the Secretary of State for Trade and Industry and the Restrictive Practices Court. Only resale price maintenance is prohibited *ab initio* (except for books and pharmaceuticals). Everything else is subject to case by case examination, either by the MMC or the Court and a practice or situation, say a merger, can only be prohibited or modified in the particular instance and if the investigation has identified effects adverse to the public interest. It is this public interest test which now distinguishes the UK from most other competition laws, including that of the European Community (EC).

The public interest is a broad, indeed nebulous, concept. If the objective of UK competition policy is to promote and maintain competition where that would enhance the public interest, it is clear that that is a wider purpose than the promotion of competition in order to enhance economic efficiency or to enhance consumer welfare. Not surprisingly, perhaps, the underlying policy governing the application of the UK legislation is therefore not always as coherent and focussed as it might be. As one French observer recently wrote about the UK system:

> 'The United Kingdom, in the light of its traditions, takes the discussion of competition problems seriously. Indeed, it has almost raised it to an art form, even if sometimes it is merely art for art's sake.'[1]

In this lecture I shall discuss my own short list of desirable improvements to UK competition law and policy. Whether my remarks count as an 'art form' I must leave to you, the audience, to judge.

International Dimension

I shall be discussing domestic law. EC competition law, Articles 85 and 86 of the Treaty of Rome and supporting regulations, is directly applicable in the UK when inter-State trade is affected. With growing international trade, the globalisation of markets and increasingly international business activity, EC law has an ever greater impact within the UK. This is well illustrated by the extension of the European Commission's jurisdiction to mergers ('concentrations' in EC parlance) which have a 'Community dimension' with the coming into force in September 1991 of the EC merger control regulation, 4064/89. International developments require close co-operation between authorities but, more, they point to the need for convergence in national laws and enforcement policies. I am glad to see that this is a priority agenda item in a number of fora including the Competition Law and Policy Committee of the OECD. Some of my suggestions for improvement in UK law would, if adopted, be a step towards such a convergence.

Restrictive Trading Agreements

The most obvious and urgent need for improvement is in the law dealing with cartels and other forms of restrictive trading agreements. An effective means of controlling blatantly anti-competitive agreements

[1.] H. Dumez and A. Jeunnemaitre, *La Concurrence en Europe*, Seuil, 1991, p.114.

2

such as price-fixing and market-sharing agreements, bid rigging and collusive tendering is a *sine qua non* for an effective competition policy and therefore for an efficiently functioning market economy. Frankly, the Restrictive Trade Practices Act is not up to the task.

The Act requires that parties to any agreement in which two or more of them accept restrictions on their commercial freedom of action must provide details of the agreement to my Office for registration before it is put into effect. Otherwise the restrictions in the agreement are void and unenforceable; in effect the agreement is unlawful. Whether or not an agreement is registrable depends upon its *form*, not upon its effects. This means that agreements can be drafted in such a way as to evade the law, for example, if only one party accepts a restriction. The law requires me to refer registrable agreements, whether lawfully or unlawfully made, to the Restrictive Practices Court. The Act presumes that the restrictions are against the public interest and if the parties are unable to demonstrate benefits (under any of a number of 'gateways' specified in the Act) which outweigh the adverse effects of the agreement, the Court will strike down the restrictions, ordering the parties not to give effect to them and, usually, not to make similar arrangements in the future. Where an agreement has not been properly notified it will usually be undefended, in which case the Court will declare the restrictions against the public interest and again make an order or take an undertaking from the parties. Details of blatant cartels are virtually never furnished to the Office as required by the Act.

It is now rare for a case to be defended before the Court - the last case concerned the ABTA reciprocal exclusive dealing agreement heard by the Court 10 years ago. Usually when details of an agreement are notified to the Office before the agreement comes into effect, I am able to use a facility provided by Section 21 of the Act (and first introduced in 1968) not to refer agreements to the Court (with the approval of the Secretary of State) if the restrictions seem too insignificant to warrant investigation by the Court. The Office is generally able to negotiate a modification of an agreement to remove any restrictions which do, in our view, have a significant effect on competition against the threat of a reference to the Court. Several hundred agreements may be dealt with in this way in a single year.

Before I comment upon the particular weaknesses of the legislation, let me hasten to say that the Restrictive Trade Practices Act is not an entirely broken reed. Indeed, year after year we do uncover secret and therefore unlawful agreements the restrictions in which are in due course declared against the public interest by the Court. Many of these cases concern materials used in the construction sector. They are certainly not confined to that sector, but it is a characteristic of most of the products (or services) involved that they serve local markets and markets little exposed to the threat of new competition and immune from competition from abroad (invariably they are cases outside the jurisdiction of the European Commission since there is unlikely to be an effect upon inter-State trade).

There are three main deficiencies in the legislation. First, the registration requirements in the Act catch a very large number of agreements which will have no effect, or certainly no significant effect, on competition. In 1991 details of no fewer than 1,327 agreements were notified to the Office. On recent experience it is likely that less than 50 per cent will be found to be registrable. Most of the rest will be found to contain no restrictions significant enough to require a reference to the Court. The processing of these agreements involves a considerable expenditure of resources within the Office, DTI and industry for very little benefit. I also recognise the force of the criticism that when decisions are reached administratively, sometimes after the removal or modification of anti-competitive restrictions by negotiation, rather than by Court proceedings, industry and its legal advisers are unlikely to be aware of the criteria used by the Office and its reasoning in a particular case. We are considering ways of meeting this criticism and we are also working on ways of streamlining our procedures. But there is no way around the basic shortcoming of the Act that it focusses attention on the form of agreements rather than upon the effects, a shortcoming that blunts its effectiveness in the control of cartels.

The second major weakness is the inadequate investigatory powers. Effectively the only power the Office has when it suspects that an unregistered agreement is in operation is to issue a Section 36 notice. This requires those upon whom it is served to give details of any registrable agreements to which they are a party. We use this power quite frequently (71 Section 36 notices were issued in 1991) but we can only issue the notice where we have 'reasonable cause to believe' that there is a registrable agreement. This phrase has been narrowly interpreted by the courts and, although there are penalties for refusing to reply or for giving false information, we have virtually no means of proceeding in the face of denials even when we continue to have legitimate suspicions. The most effective kind of investigatory power is the power to enter premises and search for evidence of a suspected agreement. The European Commission has such powers under Regulation 17/62. Some newspaper stories notwithstanding, there have been very few complaints from British industry about the Commission's use of these powers, and I do not see why they should not be part of the armoury of the UK authorities with such safeguards as that the power would only be exercisable if a court was satisfied that there were reasonable cause for suspicion. Experience in other countries, as well as that of the European Commission, demonstrates the importance of this kind of power to the effective pursuit of secret cartels. Without it, we are unduly dependent upon the chance contributions of whistle-blowers for the leads that enable us to track down unlawful registrable agreements. Commenting upon the European Commission's success in uncovering a number of cartels in the chemicals sector, Sir Leon Brittan said in a recent speech:

> 'What is absolutely clear is that without the vigorous use by the Commission of its investigatory powers, conferred by Articles 11 and 14 of Regulation 17, few of these serious cartels and monopoly abuses would ever have come to light. In several recent cases the "smoking gun" evidence was found during unannounced investigations ordered by decision and carried out simultaneously across the Community. It would certainly never have been produced on a voluntary basis by any of those involved in the clandestine activities. ...During the last ten years...the Commission has had increasingly to use such measures in investigating major cases.'[2]

The Commission can also impose large fines for violations of Article 85 (fines of up to 10 per cent of turnover). Under UK law there are no financial penalties for failure to comply with the statutory obligation to furnish details of a registrable agreement before it is put into effect. There is a ground for a private action for damages for loss suffered through breach of the statutory duty, but there have been few such actions so far. None has resulted in a court judgement and there have to my knowledge been few out-of-court settlements. A number of local authorities have been considering taking action against ready-mixed concrete and glass suppliers who have operated unlawful secret agreements, but all are encountering difficulties, I understand, in establishing in money terms

---

[2] Sir Leon Brittan, *Competition Policy and Procedures,* Address to the Centre for European Policy Studies, 16 September 1991.

the loss they have suffered. Of course I seek injunctions in the Court prohibiting further collusion and, if the order is broken, then the Court can impose unlimited fines, even imprisonment, for contempt of Court. In fact, however, the fines for contempt in cartel cases have been quite modest, even derisory compared with the fines exacted in some cases by the European Commission: ICI, for instance, were fined around £12 million in one recent case (though Sir Leon Brittan has complained that some firms regard fines 'as just another overhead').[3]

These weaknesses of the UK legislation on restrictive trading agreements have been compounded by the Court of Appeal's recent decision in *DGFT v Smiths Concrete Ltd* [1991][4] All E.R. 150, that Smiths Concrete Ltd was not a party to a price-fixing and market-sharing agreement which operated in the Bicester area although a manager in its employment had joined in the agreement with representatives of other companies. Smiths had forbidden its employees to make such an agreement. The Court held that where an employee acts outside the scope of his or her authority (albeit within the scope of his employment), his actions do not bind his employer. The employer is therefore not party to a registrable agreement and is not in contempt of any previous order of the court imposed upon the employer such as had been made some years earlier against Smiths. The House of Lords has refused me leave to appeal against the decision. While this will not dissuade us from continuing to enforce the law and from referring unlawful agreements to the Court, it is a considerable disappointment; indeed, I was surprised at the Court of Appeal's decision. But a careful reading of the judgements suggests that the effectiveness of the law may not have been weakened quite as much as might at first appear: the employer must have taken all reasonable steps (by way of adequate monitoring and compliance machinery) to make his employees aware that making or participating in registrable agreements is outside the scope of their authority if the employer is to benefit from the Court of Appeal's ruling. It is up to the employer to show that he has taken such steps in the face of evidence that an employee did make and operate agreements of the proscribed kind. Nevertheless, the Court of Appeal decision does underline the urgency of the case for reform of the UK law.

[3.] *Ibid.*

[4.] DTI, *Opening Markets: New Policy on Restrictive Trade Practices,* Cm.727, London: HMSO, July 1989.

It is unlikely that the inadequacies of the Restrictive Trade Practices Act can be put right without fundamental reform. I suppose something more limited could be done by way of enhancing OFT's investigatory powers and the introduction of financial penalties for failure to furnish details of agreements for registration. But the real need is to replace the form-based law with its registration system and public interest test with a system under which anti-competitive agreements are prohibited *ab initio* unless they meet specified criteria for an exemption from the prohibition. So long as the exemption criteria are narrow in order to allow only agreements which will improve economic efficiency and benefit consumers at least ultimately, such a system would give a clearer signal to businesses of the kinds of co-operative behaviour that were permitted and the kinds that were not acceptable. And with a prohibition system there can be no argument that enforcement requires strong investigatory powers of the kind enjoyed by the European Commission, and that firms which wilfully or flagrantly violate the law should be subject to the risk of heavy financial penalties.

The present Government's White Paper of July 1989 proposed that anti-competitive agreements and concerted practices should be prohibited but with a provision for exemption modelled on Article 85(3) of the Treaty (and also with a *de minimis* exemption). The proposals received a wide measure of support, including from most lawyers experienced in the field and, more surprisingly, from much of industry. No doubt a major reason why industry saw merit in the proposals was the advantages of closer alignment of UK and EC law. Another reason might be the scope for private actions for damages, although I would not myself expect much private enforcement, at any rate without the sort of incentive provided in the United States of treble damages for successful plaintiffs.

It is disappointing that the Government has been unable to find time in the 1977-1992 Parliament for a Bill to give effect to its White Paper proposals. I appreciate that the White Paper proposals involve much more than a strengthening of OFT's investigatory powers and the introduction of stronger penalties, not least the reconstruction of my Office as an authority with decision-making powers subject to appeal to a tribunal to be formed from the membership of the MMC - an intriguing idea this, which would cast MMC members for the first time in an appellate rôle - and ultimately to the courts. This would be a major institutional change, and it would no doubt come under close scrutiny in Parliament as and

7

when incorporated in any Bill. But I have little doubt that such an authority would be necessary for effective enforcement of a new law. It would of course require a change in the procedures and organisation of my Office with the holding of hearings, publication of reasons for our decisions and so forth - very different from the administrative procedures we follow in applying the Restrictive Trade Practices Act - and it would no doubt require a cultural change, if not at least some changes in the staffing of the Office.

All this has to be for the future. But it may have escaped the attention of many that the Broadcasting Act 1990 has anticipated implementation of the July 1989 White Paper proposals in one industry. This Act is the latest in a number of recent statutes which have extended my rôle in competition policy matters in certain sectors of the economy. Special procedures have been set up for assessing rules made by self-regulatory bodies established under the Financial Services Act 1986, and in respect of auditing and legal services under the Companies Act 1989 and the Courts and Legal Services Act 1990. Broadly, rules made by these bodies or affecting aspects of these services cannot be introduced, or changed, without a report from me to the Secretary of State, or in the case of legal services, to the Lord Chancellor, on the impact of the rules on competition. If I report that the rules would be significantly anti-competitive, it is then for the Minister to decide whether or not those adverse effects of the rules are outweighed by their contribution to investor protection, the competent and independent provision of professional services, or whatever is the purpose of the regulatory system. It is the Minister who has to do any balancing of benefits and detriments from the rules and reach a judgement, effectively on the public interest, rather than the Court as in the case of restrictive trading agreements or the MMC on other matters.

The procedures are rather different under the Broadcasting Act. Under this legislation I have to examine the networking arrangements of Channel 3 television broadcasters, that is the co-operative commissioning, scheduling and showing of programmes, and decide first whether or not they are anti-competitive and, if so, whether they are nevertheless acceptable according to criteria akin to those in Article 85(3) of the Treaty of Rome. This is the first time that the DGFT has been given the power to decide - subject to appeal to the MMC - where the public interest lies in any potentially anti-competitive arrangement. We are already embarked on this process, having had to develop in embryo the sort of procedures we would follow should the Office ever become a full-blown competition authority. My decision on networking will be of profound importance to the television industry, but it is the novelty of the rôle that I am called upon to play that may be of wider interest.

'Monopolies' and Anti-Competitive Practices

If the OFT were established as a new-style authority to deal with restrictive trading agreements, with enhanced investigatory powers, and a new decision-making rôle, it might seem odd to retain the existing laws and procedures for dealing with anti-competitive practices of individual firms with market power and with conduct amounting to the exploitation of market power.

The Competition Act empowers the DGFT to initiate an OFT investigation of any course of conduct which 'has or is intended to have or is likely to have the effect of restricting, distorting or preventing competition' within the UK or any part of it. This is a wide definition indeed of anti-competitive behaviour. No examples are given in the statute of practices that might be regarded as anti-competitive. Nor is there any statutory requirement that an enterprise be dominant or have some stated minimum market share before a Competition Act investigation can be set in motion. If the OFT concludes that an enterprise has engaged in an anti-competitive practice it may offer undertakings to the DGFT to remedy the adverse effects. Absent satisfactory undertakings, the DGFT may make a competition reference to the MMC, when they must first say whether or not they find the practice anti-competitive and, if so, whether or not it operates against the public interest. Only if the MMC make such a finding are there statutory powers to prohibit or modify the offending practice.

Despite the two-stage investigatory procedure, the Competition Act was seen as providing a speedier and more effective way of dealing with anti-competitive behaviour than traditional monopoly references. Under the Fair Trading Act the DGFT is empowered to refer 'monopoly situations' to the MMC. These exist where 25 per cent or more of the supply of any good or service in the UK or in a part of it is accounted for by one enterprise or, with a 'complex monopoly situation', where a group of enterprises which together account for 25 per cent or more are behaving in a way that has the effect of preventing, restricting or distorting competition. The discretion to make a monopoly reference is a wide one, though in practice I shall always be looking for some *prima facie* evidence of the misuse or exploitation of market power before invoking the statute. And the scope of the MMC's investigation is also wide. Unless expressly limited by their terms of reference, the MMC are to look into all aspects of the monopoly situation, to report whether any 'acts or omissions' of the relevant parties operate against the public interest and, if desired, to make recommendations as to how the adverse effects might be remedied. The Secretary of State has extensive order-making powers to remedy any identified adverse effects, though usually he will ask the DGFT to obtain voluntary undertakings from the parties. Remedies have invariably focussed on market behaviour of enterprises rather than directly on the structure of the market(s) in which the firm operates. This and the fact that monopoly investigation in the 1970s typically lasted two or three years, led the Government to introduce the Competition Act procedures following a recommendation of the Liesner review committee in their reports in 1978 and 1979.[5]

This part of the competition legislation has not been as successful as was hoped. The OFT have no powers to obtain information under the Competition Act before a formal investigation is launched, and our only power under the Fair Trading Act is to require information that would assist us to determine whether or not a monopoly situation exists. We have no power to demand information about market behaviour or profitability. The result is that we are very dependent upon complaints. Yet these are a very imperfect guide to the sources of market failure and as often as not concern small or local market situations. There have been far fewer Competition Act investigations than envisaged and the procedures, up to the stage of any reference to the MMC, have been more protracted than anticipated and compare unfavourably with monopoly references which in recent times have usually been completed in one year or less.

From the point of view of businessmen, a major criticism of the legislation is the lack of legal certainty. Firms do not know sufficiently clearly the circumstances that may prompt an investigation or the likely outcome of an investigation. From the authorities' point of view the wide

[5] Reviews of *Monopolies and Mergers Policy and of Restrictive Trade Practices Policy,* Consultative Documents, Cmnd.7198, May 1978, and Cmnd.7512, March 1979.

scope of the legislation undoubtedly has its attractions, but we do have some reservations about its effectiveness. The remedies secured after an investigation apply only to the firms involved in that investigation; they do not establish precedents in the legal sense and they are likely to have only a limited impact upon the conduct of other firms in other markets. The deterrent effect of the system is limited.

From both points of view I therefore think there would be merit in considering the adoption of a law similar to Article 86 of the Treaty of Rome which prohibits any conduct that amounts to an abuse of a dominant position. There would still be uncertainty, not least because of the arguments that would ensue over market definition and whether an enterprise was dominant, and doubts about what conduct might constitute an abuse. But this would diminish as case law which would establish legal precedent developed, as has occurred in the Community, and existing Community precedents would also be of some value.

The main advantage of a change would be more effective enforcement. Not only would it be appropriate for the authority to have similar investigatory powers as for the investigation of suspected cartels but there would also be the possibility of interim measures and fines in appropriate cases. Consider a case of predatory pricing: under UK law it is impossible to take any remedial action until the close of an investigation, and then the likeliest remedy would be either an undertaking not to predate again or an undertaking to fix prices in future according to a formula or other criterion agreed with the authorities, a remedy which clearly could have the perverse effect of restricting rather than promoting competitive behaviour. Under an Article 86 type of system, interim measures could be taken while the allegation was being investigated and if an abuse of market power was confirmed the predator could be fined; if he repeated the offence he could be fined again but more heavily. Other firms would then more readily learn the score, and the greater deterrent to predatory behaviour is obvious. The main disadvantage is that appeals against the decision of the authority can extend the time-scales considerably (and provide a field day for lawyers).

A law which prohibits the abuse of a dominant position, or more generally the abuse of market power, is directed at the conduct of enterprises. It is particularly suited to dealing with anti-competitive conduct, whether predatory or exclusionary. This has been the provenance of the Competition Act. The abuse of dominant position approach seems less well suited to dealing with conduct amounting to the exploitation of market power, the charging of 'excessive' prices. The examination of this possibility has often been a feature of monopoly references to the MMC and has to my mind been a useful aspect of UK procedures. Of course, there is no need to worry about excessive profits if entry into the market is easy. But entry barriers may be such as to rule out the prospect of effective competition from newcomers in the foreseeable future. If there is no practical way to reduce entry barriers, the alternative remedies are stark: forcible break-up of the dominant firm or some form of price or profits regulation. The Fair Trading Act does give the Secretary of State powers to dismember enterprises or require divestment but if there are economies of scale in an industry, break-up of a dominant firm could lead to efficiency losses; and the MMC may also have in mind that competition will not be much enhanced unless the restructuring is of major dimensions. Whatever the reasons, the MMC's usual remedy in the case of an entrenched dominant firm has been regulation of prices or profits, most recently in the case of white salt. I would favour the retention of a power to make monopoly references side by side with a law prohibiting the abuse of a dominant position. The various special regulatory régimes set up under the privatisation statutes for telecommunications, airports, gas, electricity and water all involve regulation of prices or profits and all can, or must, involve the MMC in the regulatory process. Later lecturers in this series will be discussing these régimes in some detail. Let me just say that there are already some difficulties from the interface between those régimes and the general competition law, best illustrated by the case of British Gas. There is an argument that what I called elsewhere 'a patchwork of agencies and regulatory instruments'[6] will itself require rationalisation in the not too distant future. Any reforms of the Fair Trading Act and the Competition Act would surely bring issues to the forefront.

Mergers

I have left to last a few remarks on merger control, a subject big and controversial enough to deserve a lecture in its own right. The Secretary of State has a larger rôle in this than in other parts of UK competition

---

6. G. Borrie, 'Office of Fair Trading: Reflections on Regulation', in C. Veljanovski (ed.), *Regulators and the Market,* IEA Readings No.35, London: Institute of Economic Affairs, 1991, p.92.

policy. He decides whether any qualifying merger should be referred to the MMC, though he must have regard to the advice of the DGFT on the question, and it is then for the MMC to investigate and report whether the merger, or the merger proposal, operates or may be expected to operate against the public interest. The statutory burden of proof that governs the MMC is that it may make an adverse finding only if it is satisfied that the merger operates or may be expected to operate against the public interest. It is not for the takeover bidder or the parties to the merger to prove that the merger may be expected to operate in the public interest. Where the MMC do find against it the Secretary of State can prevent a merger either by order or by taking undertakings or he can allow it subject to modifications or conditions. Under the Companies Act 1989, undertakings to divest part of a business may be accepted, without a reference to the MMC, where they would eradicate any adverse effects. This is an important development in the law but can only be activated in practice in a small number of cases. Mergers, which are broadly defined in the Fair Trading Act, qualify for reference if the gross assets acquired are £30 million or more, or if 25 per cent 'market share' is created or enhanced in the UK or a 'substantial part' of it (the authorities' interpretation of 'substantial part' in the South Yorkshire Transport case has been overturned following judicial review of an MMC report; a decision whether to appeal to the House of Lords is pending).

The Trade and Industry Select Committee of the House of Commons has recently reported on mergers policy.[7] The main policy issue to emerge from the Committee's deliberations is whether the policy of the Government as regards the grounds on which a merger should be referred to the MMC should be broadened. For some years, under the so-called 'Tebbit doctrine', the policy of the Secretary of State has been that the primary consideration should be the effect of mergers upon competition, with other matters only exceptionally being relevant. The Select Committee were equally divided as to whether reference policy should continue to be based mainly on competition grounds. These are matters for government policy. Because of the breadth of the public interest test in Section 84 of the Fair Trading Act, a change would not need any amendment to the legislation though a change of policy may not be very effective without an amendment to the statutory burden of proof that governs the MMC's

---

[7] Trade and Industry Committee, First Report, *Take Overs and Mergers*, HC 90, 27 November 1991.

deliberations. I believe that my Office should work within the parameters of both the law and the publicly declared policy of government but, as we are principally concerned with actual and potential threats to competition, I feel it is appropriate to propose a particular change in the statutory burden of proof myself. I want to raise the hurdle to be surmounted before an anti-competitive merger could be allowed. In particular, I think the law should make clear that a merger which had non-trivial adverse effects upon competition within any UK market should not be allowed unless, on examination by the MMC, they had concluded that there were benefits, benefits which would only occur if the merger took place, which clearly offset the detriments to competition. This might seem more a change of stance than substance, but I feel it would give a clearer signal than now that anti-competitive mergers invariably operate against the public interest. Those who claim mergers are necessary to exploit economies of scale or to improve international competitiveness should expect to have to justify those claims if competition would be reduced by the merger.

On the whole, I think the Fair Trading Act system of merger control, including the institutional machinery, is reasonably satisfactory. Critics, including the Select Committee, have argued that reference policy could be made more predictable if the Secretary of State gave fuller reasons for his decisions, including decisions not to refer, and if guidelines on the criteria used by OFT in our scrutiny of mergers were published. I would not wish the system to be any more secretive than it need be, and I suggest that those with experience of the system are very well aware of the factors that OFT takes into account, always accepting that there can be argument about the effects of a merger on competition in any particular case, whatever any published guidelines may say.[8] There have also been a number of administrative improvements to the system in recent years, notably a significant shortening of the time taken for the MMC's investigation. One area where some further improvement is nevertheless desirable is in the time taken to complete divestments, whether required as an alternative to a reference or as a result of an MMC investigation. Because of the new power to accept legally enforceable undertakings instead of making a reference to the MMC, and because a number of completed mergers have been referred in the last few years, the OFT has become more involved in the negotiation and subsequent implementation

---

[8.] OFT also publish a guide, *Mergers: A Guide to the Procedures under the Fair Trading Act*, 1991.

of divestments of businesses or parts of businesses. It is a matter of some concern that divestments can take many weeks (even months) to bring about. This suggests that tighter deadlines should probably be set and those deadlines enforced, if necessary, by statutory order or action in the courts, notwithstanding the possible commercial consequences of a forced sale.

Conclusion

As I said at the outset, UK competition law is complex. While I naturally believe in the benefits to society from an active competition policy, I do recognise a number of shortcomings of the present system. I have concentrated primarily on the weaknesses of the UK law on restrictive trading agreements, for it is in that area that the case for reform is, in my view, overwhelming and urgent. I have been pressing for reform of the Restrictive Trade Practices Act for some years so I have taken the opportunity in this lecture to give you some of my thoughts about other areas where our law or policy might be improved. Whatever else their merits, I am sure that they would bring about a useful simplification of the present law and a sharper focus of the policy in furtherance of which the law is applied.

HOW CAN UK COMPETITION POLICY BE IMPROVED?

DISCUSSANT:

Mr. Thomas Sharpe

Barrister

THE OFFICE OF FAIR TRADING is very largely Sir Gordon Borrie's creation and his long and successful tenure as Director General has marked a number of important developments which reinforce the case he has deployed for an urgent review of the complex structure of UK competition legislation. Complexity, of itself, is seldom sufficient to justify review and it may be sensible to begin this comment by describing the principal developments since 1976.

First, the UK has established itself as a member of the European Community. At the same time, Articles 85 and 86 have become familiar, especially to the larger elements of British industry. In addition, the EC Commission's initiatives under Article 90(3) have had an impact in regulating the conduct of publicly owned enterprises in their relationship with governments and also on various sectors, such as telecommunications. EC competition laws do not merely mean the enforcement of Articles 85 and 86 by the EC Commission, including the adoption of Regulations on sectors such as beer, petrol distribution and cars; although this is important, it also means the ability to apply Articles 85 and 86 in national courts to seek a remedy in damages or injunction.

For most large companies and for many smaller ones with an export or import trade with other member-states, or for undertakings which enter into a network of agreements within the United Kingdom which, taken together, may affect competition and trade, EC competition law is of more importance than domestic UK competition law, especially as the relevant EC law is directly effective in the UK courts.

The UK authorities must also have regard to EC competition laws. For example, in the course of the MMC inquiry into motor cars it was apparent that there were many aspects of motor dealer distribution agreements which had been sanctioned as compatible with Regulation 123/85 and which therefore were presumptively enforceable as compatible with Article 85(1). The view was expressed to the MMC by many motor companies that the UK authorities had no jurisdiction to impose stricter obligations than those contained in Regulation 123/85. The Secretary of State's rôle in such matters had to be confined to making representations to the EC Commission that account should be taken of his views, deriving from the MMC report and other sources, in any revision of the Commission regulation.

There is a strong case, therefore, for any change in UK competition law to reflect what has now become familiar in British industry, namely, the law and practice of the European Community. [Since the lecture, this option has been put forward for discussion by the DTI in relation to abuses of dominant positions, thus mirroring the proposed changes to the restrictive practices régime discussed by Sir Gordon.]

The second important change which took place during Sir Gordon's régime was the privatisation programme and the advent of licensing régimes for the formerly publicly owned utilities to be supervised by regulators. Here, there are two régimes in play: first, the specific regulatory structure for each industry; secondly, the general competition law found in the Fair Trading Act 1973, Competition Act 1980 and Restrictive Practices Act 1976. It is moot whether in the context of stronger laws relating to 'abuse' it would be necessary to continue to have specific competition provisions in each sector. Moreover, changing and liberalised structures have spawned new areas of concern, for example, in buses, following from deregulation, in milk, after the demise or rebadging of the MMB, or in coal procurement and supply after the privatisation of the two main electricity generators.

The third change I want to identify is that brought about by the changing structure of industry. The reduction in the proportion of output represented by manufacturing brings into relief the competition issues raised by new technology and the service sector, including transport. In some areas (satellites is one example), new technology has created new sources of competition and has thus expanded the relevant market for analysis. In other areas (for example, buses), it is arguable that competition policy has been insensitive to the need for some co-ordination and co-operation. Entertainment and broadcasting are other areas where some initiatives have been taken. The innovation regarding network agreements and their scrutiny by the OFT in accordance with a formula which owes everything to Article 85(3) is an early precursor of the convergence between UK and EC law discussed above. But restrictions on film material and on franchisees may, and usually do, escape any competition scrutiny.

Turning now to the substance of UK competition policy, there are many weaknesses. It is hard to identify whether the UK economy is more or less competitive as a result of any Act of Parliament as opposed to the existence of competitors. The main source of competition has been from imports and this has occasionally been sudden and destructive. Sectors which are largely free of imports may be less competitive but I know of no evidence in support of this proposition. I know of inconclusive data on the degree of concentration in the British economy but I cannot infer from that data whether the concentrated sectors are any more or less competitive than less concentrated sectors or whether behaviour would be any different if the competition laws were any different, either as to mergers or as to unilateral behaviour in the past. I do know, from my own experience, that UK cartel laws are largely avoidable and are long overdue for reform. Indeed, it is surprising that Conservative governments, which have placed such a premium on the operation of competitive forces to achieve certain solutions, should have refused to underwrite the process by clearly drafted prohibitions and familiar enforcement procedures. The proposed changes in cartel laws fall far short of the clear expression of policy which is required in order to educate a new generation of businessmen. Moreover, the proposed rôle of the MMC in adjudicating cases and enforcing penalties is curious given the rôle of the ordinary courts in hearing Article 85 cases and also in hearing any proposed private actions under the new régime. The MMC's great strength is its detachment from enforcement and the depth with which it can investigate industry situations. Adjudication between the appellant and the decision of the OFT will be an unfamiliar activity for the MMC and does not build on any obvious strength possessed by the MMC. Its chief attraction would seem to be that the MMC is not a 'court', although it is hard to see what comfort that fact will offer to undertakings facing financial penalties and exposure to private actions.

Sir Gordon does not put much faith in private proceedings in the absence of any incentives, such as treble damages. This has been the experience under the provisions of the restrictive practices legislation since private actions were possible from 1968. A more accurate indicator might be the rôle of the courts in applying Articles 85 and 86 throughout the EC. The courts have been active in developing concepts such as the relevant market, predation, concerted practice, dominance, discrimination, market power, occasionally seeking guidance from the Court of Justice by way of references under Article 177. This has led to the development of doctrine on these key issues and others. It is hard to identify the contribution of the UK authorities to a better understanding of these ideas. While seeking to be consistent, the MMC has seldom spelt out analytically what is meant by market power and other concepts, yet these concepts are unavoidably applied in each report. I should add that this public failure may not have affected the quality of the reports as, plainly, the notions are employed by the Commissioners and staff. It does make it more difficult to identify in advance the interpretation the MMC will apply to particular situations and this is so even if the facts and matters central to each inquiry are completely understood by a reading of each report, which is not always the case.

The failure to articulate a consistent doctrine on each of the key elements of competition law has been the greatest failure of UK policy since 1948 and in any justification that each case must be treated on its merits fails to address the importance of being able to identify in advance or to advise in advance that certain behaviour is lawful or not. If this task is not undertaken the OFT and MMC have free rein over every fact-situation which would be dealt with as part of a 'wilderness of single instances'. The MMC has taken steps to make its pronouncements more consistent and they are to be welcomed. But the MMC can only work within the legislative framework and this framework, for example, does not invite them to consider expressly whether an undertaking has 'market power' (an essential preliminary for any inquiry) or even what the relevant market would be.

Private actions would appear to introduce deterrence, compensation and education to UK competition policy and thus serve to refine the notions which are essential to the broader public law question of official enforcement under whatever régime is adopted.

COMMON CARRIER REGULATION

Sir James McKinnon
Director General, OFGAS

Introduction

THE TITLE IS intriguing. When I saw it first, I thought about the various types of common carriers which exist and began to speculate whether there was an element of regulation associated with each one. There were buses, trains, aircraft and taxis, they are common carriers to be sure; there are conductors, guards, cabin staff and drivers, but does that make these worthy people regulators or their job regulation? No, they are part of the service being provided by the owner of the carriage business. In any event, I doubt if a conductor on the legendary Clapham Omnibus would see himself as a regulator. Given the image of a regulator, if you referred to him in that way, you would probably end up on the pavement.

In examining this topic I believe I have just made the most important point that I can. The operations involved in the common carrier process represent a service. In all the service businesses in which I have been involved, such as hotels, restaurants and pubs, I have found that you can only be successful if you really want to give a service and all the people who work for you feel the same. It is perfectly true that you must observe the law in providing the service. Well, perhaps there have been a few pub tenants or managers who have failed to observe the licensing hours as rigidly as they should; it was probably their burning desire to serve which affected either their judgement or their eyesight. In every service business the safety of the users of the service is the one element which can never be compromised.

There are service companies which are monopolies or quasi-monopolies. In my experience I have never found a monopolist who has volunteered to reduce the level of his profitability. If such a thing happens I find it is as a result of external pressure. This is an understandable situation - certainly I understand it having been employed by a monopolist for a number of years. That particular monopoly was broken as a result of EC regulations becoming effective in Britain. I speculate on the energy monopolies of Europe and wonder whether their situations within the EC will ever be affected by the introduction of regulations of a type which first saw the light of day in Britain. If it is recognised that there is likely to be reluctance on the part of the owner of facilities to provide a service and that owner regards the use of the assets as an imposition, there can be no question of viewing the operations as the provision of a service. A different approach has to be taken.

The Monopoly Aspect

It is at this point we depart from the bus service type of business and enter the sphere of common carrier regulation. We move into a similar situation as exists in the tariff segment of the gas supply market; we have to have surrogate competition to make things work. The regulator becomes the surrogate competitor and will attempt to secure a level of prices and workable contract terms for all third parties who wish to use the facilities owned by a monopolist. The fact that a regulator is needed can be illustrated by the gas supply market where common carriage became legally possible in 1982 but took place in 1990, mainly as a result of the intervention of the regulator.

It seemed to come as a surprise to a number of people that it became possible for third parties to make use of the gas pipelines in Britain by which to deliver product to their customers. No doubt they were equally surprised that there was competitive activity in the first place. They should have read the Gas Act 1986. There are still those in Continental Europe who say that it is impossible. But some people say that it is aerodynamically impossible for bees to fly but they still manage to collect the pollen they need. Common carriage is a fact of life in the utility scene in Britain, it happens in the USA, so are there factors unique to these countries which are absent in the European situation? No, it is the presence of competition which forces common carriage to be undertaken. The European monopolies may not wish to embrace change, but they will have to be like Lord Nelson, when he put the telescope to his blind eye, not to get the message. It is possible.

The Fears About Common Carriage

Perhaps the feeling in Europe is based on a series of misunderstandings. As far as I can follow the arguments, these suggest that there will be inevitable dangers to security of supply and that the operations of the businesses will become more expensive. It has also been suggested that such costs will have to be passed on to the final users of the delivery systems. A more general assertion has been made that in relation to gas there will be a diminution of exploration activity and a reduction in investment levels.

If these allegations are well founded, it is strange that they have not manifested themselves in the USA or in Britain. It may be an opportune time to examine the elements of the claims in the light of what has happened in the gas supply industry in Britain. This is particularly apposite when almost all of these aspects have been raised by British Gas as being direct results of the undertakings required by OFT in regard to the acceleration of competition in the gas supply business. It seems that whenever the profitability of a monopolist is threatened these points are raised. If they are valid the price of competition will be too high.

Let us consider the various contentions made. Perhaps the most vital is that common carriage will pose a threat to security of supply. At the moment there is an adequate supply of gas flowing from the North Sea based on a series of contracts and the need for a common carriage procedure surely cannot affect the physical presence of the gas or the contract. The pipelines will remain in existence and the thing that will change is the number of companies making use of these facilities. Can it be that the operators of the pipelines will be unable to cope with instructions from a number of sources? In the light of the sophistication of information technology today, surely this cannot be so.

When it is possible for a traveller to walk into a small shop in a one-street town in the Rockies with a request to re-route his journey to London via Hong Kong and Singapore using two different carriers and being able

23

to leave in a few minutes with a confirmed booking and seat reservations, the problems of routeing supplies of gas are surely surmountable. When you consider furthermore that the necessary debits and credits between airlines will also have been secured you may agree that the technical capability exists easily to support common carriage without danger to security of supply.

As far as additional costs are concerned, it is appropriate to ask where these are likely to arise and for whose account. Common carriage will be required as competition develops. These competitors will incur new costs and as they arise there will be a diminution in the costs of the monopolist. The competitors will gain income; the monopolist will shed it on sales but retain income from carriage operations. The beneficiaries will be the customers and competitors and the loser will be the monopolist. As prices to end-users fall there is a strong probability that volumes of sales will rise. The extra costs, if any, will be investments in information technology upgrading, capital investments recovered by amortisation, and internal efficiencies. Frankly I find it difficult to see the sources of additional costs; but if they do arise they are not going to be of such significance as to cause prices to rise to the end-users.

The reason for operators' participation in the production of gas or the generation of electricity can be fairly said to be the pursuit of profit capable of being sustained in the long term. It may also be said that monopolists have the same idea. I do not feel able to talk about electricity but natural gas is a commodity in great demand and that demand has a good prospect of growing. The prospects for gas producers are surely related to the growth of the market for the product and will not be inhibited by the need for common carriage agreements. Competition has begun in the gas supply market and shows clear indications of growing in Britain. The one thing which is certain is that investment by producers in the North Sea in exploration and production facilities will continue to grow at a reasonable rate. This appears to rebut the claim that investment and exploration will fall if the procedures associated with common carriage come into play.

It is for each person to accept or reject the various arguments. All I can say is that a number of competitors in Britain have made up their minds.

There have been authoritative reports and statements from well-respected sources which support the claims of those opposed to the concepts of competition and common carriage. They point to the fact that there are special circumstances in Britain and the USA which are not present in the Continental European situation. They say that it is incorrect to assume the ability to transplant a system from one country to another. They are right to make such statements; the USA is different from Britain, but then the systems in operation in these two countries also differ. To try to reproduce slavishly a method operating in another country is seldom, if ever, rewarded with success. The secret of making the transition is to examine the dynamics and characteristics of the industrial position in both countries and compare and contrast the finding. There will undoubtedly be differences - some will be major and some will be minor. It may be discovered that there is a showstopper among the list of major differences. If that turns out to be the case the first thing to do is to thank your lucky stars that you found out in time. I sincerely hope that I am not one of the innocents. Furthermore, if someone knows why a transition cannot be made by the general approach to common carriage taken in Britain to another suitably prepared environment then I would dearly like to be let in on the secret. I have certainly asked often enough to be enlightened. Perhaps it will be tonight that I will find out the error of my ways.

The Competition Connection

All that said, it is certainly my feeling that, with the proper preparation, common carriage can work and can back up the benefits that can be obtained by replacing a monopoly by a self-sustaining competitive market. I have spent time in examining why it is that I believe common carriage is a perfectly workable proposition. You may or may not agree that I have made a plausible case.

If it is not feasible to introduce competition or indeed it is illegal to do so, then the whole concept of common carriage regresses to the list of trivial pursuits. There are proponents of the retention of the monopoly but you will not find them among the ranks of users of the product or service which is controlled by the monopolist. Once you accept competition in the utility area you have to accept the concept of common carriage. It would not be sensible to introduce an entirely new set of delivery facilities side by side with existing ones. It would indeed be interesting to examine the arguments in favour of such a proposition. That is not to say that competition in delivery facilities should be ruled out. On the contrary, if

25

there are new developments which will beneficially expand the market and a competition to provide facilities ensues, this can only be in the best interests of the ultimate users of the product being hauled.

At this point there may be at least a number in the audience who are in favour of competition, believe that it is inappropriate to replicate existing systems and by extension accept that common carriage arrangements are necessary. I would then contend that, as one main set of facilities will be in use, a powerful monopoly will be controlling the operation. In that event, the case for the introduction of a regulatory mechanism will be overwhelming. Which is the point at which the Gas Act 1986 came in.

The situation in regard to competitive activity has changed beyond measure in Britain from a situation in which there were loud complaints that there was no possibility of competition being introduced to the complaints of today that it is not happening nearly fast enough. We shall see a faster development over the next three years than past experience has provided. The intervention of OFT has ensured that. As the pace of competition increases the pressure on the common carriage process will become much greater than in past years. It would be helpful to review what has happened since 1990 and the creation of a method of regulating common carriage in Britain.

The Gas Act 1986

As has been indicated earlier, the Gas Act is the piece of legislation which has provided the regulator with the means by which the pipelines can be used by third parties. There are a number of concepts which are included in the legislation which provide considerable comfort both to the owner of the facilities and the end-user at one and the same time.

First of all, the Act gives the very broad hint to the owner, who is described as 'the public gas supplier', that he should really try very hard to strike a bargain with the third party that would prevent that party from calling the regulator into the discussions. It was perhaps inevitable that such an intervention would take place, but more of that later. It is made clear that only product of acceptable specification could be accepted into the system, which safeguards the operational integrity of the system and preserves the lifespan of the hardware itself.

One of the key elements which gives joint protection to both the owner of the facilities and the end-user is the rule covering access to the pipeline system in terms of loading. The operator of the pipeline has an assurance that he can negotiate with a third party on the basis that he will not be required to haul product if to do so would result in the interference with carriage arrangements arising from a previously negotiated contract for the sale of gas. Vitally, the sales include those to the tariff market. They also embrace quantities of gas which may be expected to be supplied in the future to tariff customers. Thus the public gas supplier has the right to reserve pipeline space in regard to estimates of growth which he calculates for the tariff segment. It must be said that the regulator is positioned to challenge these estimates, although he must be very careful to carry out his own duties in respect of the tariff customers.

The interests of those who have established rights to have gas conveyed must take precedence over the requests from new sources. This seems to me to be perfectly fair and is a feature which I would favour for inclusion in any set of rules which were to be constructed for a common carriage system. A point of interest in this aspect is the way in which carriage to existing customers will be viewed. It will be seen that if British Gas loses a customer to one of its competitors there will be no change in the volume of gas being carried by the pipeline system. There will merely be a transfer of sales value. Thus, it will only be in the case of a major upswing in the demand from the tariff segment or the emergence of an incremental demand from a new quarter which will cause these provisions to become effective.

As it happens, a relatively unforeseen incremental demand has emerged in Britain fairly recently, namely, the use of gas in the generation of electricity. The volumes of product in this segment of the market are fairly massive and it may have been expected that the third parties involved would have fallen foul of the provisions mentioned above. That they have been able to make satisfactory carriage arrangements is entirely due to the length of the time-scales involved in this aspect of the market. Contracts for the supply of gas have to be in place at least two years ahead of the commencement of power generation. This will provide the opportunity to enhance the pipeline system so that it will be able to accommodate the additional load which will arise. This type of approach should provide reassurance that security of supply would not be prejudiced by the introduction of common carriage.

There is one further incentive contained in the British legislation which should encourage the owner of the system to arrive at a satisfactory agreement with the third party. If he fails to complete the negotiation to the satisfaction of the third party and the regulator becomes involved in the discussions, the owner will find himself on the outside of the negotiations and will have to accept the ruling of the regulator in terms of the prices to be charged and the supply conditions contained in the carriage contract. His alternative to acceptance is the pursuit of redress by way of judicial review proceedings.

The OFGAS Intervention

As it happened, in the initial stages of the operation of the Gas Act provisions, British Gas did not find it possible to agree with the first applicant for access rights to the system and the opportunity presented itself for the third party to request that the regulator should intervene.

This situation provided a basis for discussion between OFGAS and British Gas as to how the legislation would operate in practice, since up till that time there had been no practical case to examine. These discussions were fairly protracted and they produced a result, but it was a result which had not been foreseen. A carriage contract was developed by OFGAS which was to the satisfaction of the third party and somewhat grudgingly accepted by British Gas. A happy ending you may say? Regrettably no, for the third party found to his dismay that the source of gas seemed to have evaporated and no business was done.

What did come out of this first attempt to achieve third-party access was a set of guidelines which were published by OFGAS. These were accepted by British Gas which published its terms and a set of indicative tariffs for common carriage. By doing so the monopolist had signalled acknowledgement that third-party access had become a reality in Britain. However, almost a year was to elapse before the first gas owned by a third party passed through the British Gas pipelines on its way to a non-British Gas customer.

These early discussions have proved to be useful even although the transactions were small in number and covered simple point-to-point trading. The guidelines have remained by and large intact and have benefitted from a number of innovations introduced by British Gas. Although the guidelines were rudimentary it may be helpful to review them briefly as they represent a set of basic concepts which had to be developed in the circumstances of the British gas supply industry of the early 1990s.

These are the main features which we have had to address as we at OFGAS have built up our position on common carriage.

1. We urged third-party applicants to make every effort to agree as much as possible of the arrangements with British Gas, preferably to reach total agreement, but to keep the matters referred to us to the minimum.

2. We made it clear that, although we had access to full data, we would not disclose British Gas material to the applicant.

3. The third party had the assurance that any contract would rank *pari passu* with all other British Gas contractual arrangements.

4. Almost from the start of the OFGAS operation we had been building a model of the British Gas financial position. We had agreed with British Gas a broad methodology whereby costs, revenues and investment levels would be allocated to the various activities of the company. The framework of this process was the published accounts of the company, thereby ensuring consistency of approach whether we were dealing with tariff, industrial or carriage matters. The financials of the pipeline system were available to us and we were able to come to a view of costs of various carriage tasks.

5. In individual cases we are able to identify those parts of the British Gas pipeline system which will be used by the third party and the return on these assets. An element is added in respect of a share of administration costs to arrive at the basis of the charge for use of the assets.

6. In arriving at the rate of return in respect of the assets used by the applicant we had regard to the rate of return earned by British Gas on its total gas supply business, but not only that. We also took into account returns earned by specialist pipeline operators in other parts of the world with specific risk/reward relationships applicable in that category of business.

The prices which the third party has to bear are obviously of prime interest to him. When we were considering these issues, many commentators observed that, whilst prices were important, it would probably be on the contract conditions that the common carriage proposition would fail. We were very aware of this danger, largely from the attitudes which had been displayed by British Gas to the applicants at the initial stages of the negotiations.

We approached this aspect of the determination from the following standpoint. We established, first of all, the standards which British Gas sought to attain in respect of the operation of its pipeline system. We thus were able to ensure that British Gas could not require a third party to perform to a level which British Gas itself was not prepared to attain. This process also enabled us to compare British Gas requirements with the capability of an applicant to match the British Gas standards. If we were satisfied that the applicant was unable to improve his capability we reserved the right to require British Gas to accept the best efforts of the applicant.

Whilst we were prepared to call on British Gas to accept some degree of operational shortfall by the third party, we believed it to be right for British Gas to be compensated financially for its effort. By this means OFGAS sought to make sure that competition was not inhibited for reasons of differences in operational capability between competitors and British Gas.

Examples of the type of transaction covered by the situation just described are as follows:

o   Balancing input and offtake.

o   Ceilings on input and offtake.

o   Evenness of offtake.

It is fair to say that it has been possible for British Gas and the third parties to deal with these relatively minor matters as experience has been gained. However, the fact that they were issues initially, demonstrated the rigidity which was displayed by both the applicants and British Gas at the start of this process.

A topic which enjoyed a high profile in the early days of the common carriage debate was back-up gas. The commentators, who were forecasting that if price did not halt progress, the failure to agree supply terms would, seemed to take comfort from the thought that if neither of these two stopped the show there would be no way past the barrier of back-up gas. Not that anyone could blame them for taking that position.

In the initial stage of the development of competition the quantity of gas which was available for the purpose was microscopic. A competitor who has a single source of supply only is extremely vulnerable if he has no back-up supply available. If no such supply source existed he would have no credibility as a reputable supplier. The Gas Act nominates British Gas as the provider of back-up gas.

When this is viewed in the light of normal business practice it seems most unfair on the party providing back-up. Not only is he losing a customer, he has to make his own delivery system available to a competitor to enable this to happen. It may be seen as adding insult to injury if in addition he has to make product available to his competitor. However, we all know that the world is not a fair place, so in the interest of developing competition this has to be done.

OFGAS was anxious to avoid the back-up situation being exploited by a competitor and so we called on the competitor to take all reasonable steps to avoid the need to call for back-up. We called for him to schedule known requirements for the summer season and sought to make it financially unattractive for a competitor to make habitual use of the facility. In the final analysis, if British Gas were to believe that a competitor was trying to gain undue advantage we made provision to introduce an arbiter.

The Way Forward

These then were the preliminary concepts which we sought to put in place and, although they have creaked a bit, they have not collapsed as the level of competition has risen and the amount of common carriage has grown as a consequence.

The situation is nothing if not dynamic and the investigation which has been completed by OFT has created an entirely new dimension to competitive activity. The announcement by OFT in regard to the acceleration of competition, namely, that British Gas will have to cede share in the industrial market to the extent that its residual position in 1995 will be no higher than 40 points is outstandingly good news for the gas user.

As a result of this initiative by OFT the entire basis of common carriage will have to be considered in terms of the prices charged for hauling product and in regard to the types of common carriage contract which will be needed. OFGAS has been examining this position for over a year. We are satisfied that the basic concepts which we originally developed will remain. However, let us consider the probable future position.

In accordance with the undertakings given to OFT by BG there will be a release of gas by BG to its competitors. The extent of this release will be considerable. The speed with which product will be made available to accelerate competition will mean that common carriage will expand accordingly. If competitors gain market share to the level of 60 percentage points it means that they will be supplying around 60 per cent of the volume taken by interruptible customers. At the present time no such customers are in receipt of competitive gas and, by extension of that, no common carriage arrangements relate to that strand of the market.

We foresee that a new dimension of carriage contract will have to emerge and we look forward to becoming involved in its successful development. Additionally, the OFT has decreed that British Gas will be required to segregate its transactions involving transmission and distribution of gas. It will have to make these arrangements, including pricing, totally transparent, and the pricing will have to be at arm's length. British Gas will have to ensure that its own marketing arms - and this will include sales to the tariff market - pay for the carriage of gas at the same rates as other users of the pipeline system.

The difficulties associated with this process should not be underestimated but we at OFGAS will do all in our power to assist OFT in securing the benefits they seek. The most effective way in which we can do so is by using the powers we have been given by the Gas Act in terms of regulating common carriage.

COMMON CARRIER REGULATION

DISCUSSANT:
Professor Martin Cave
Brunel University

SIR JAMES MCKINNON is quite right in pointing to the importance of common carriage regulation to the development of competition. I also agree with him that there is a natural tendency for parties required to offer common carriage services or regulators linked closely to them to dwell at perhaps excessive length on the difficulties and dangers associated with this form of entry. Where I disagree with him is principally over the difficulty or ease of establishing equitable and efficient prices for common carriage services. Even here I claim only that it is impossible to get it absolutely right, but not that hard to get it approximately right. I also believe it is almost inevitable that the regulator will get involved in this process.

Let me begin by making a critical distinction between what I shall call 'pure' common carriage and - perhaps better than 'impure' - rivalrous common carriage. Common carriage normally comes into existence because of the economies associated with aggregating traffic over a range. Thus a bus achieves considerable economies of scale up to a point, but not normally up to a point where a single vehicle satisfies the whole market. Hence in many cases we can rely on competition, supplemented by rules prohibiting discrimination, to regulate the market - despite Sir Gordon Borrie's recent regret at the absence of an Ofbus. But common carriage really becomes a regulatory issue in the network industries where the costs of duplication rule out, for the short term at least, the equivalent of entry of a rival bus service. The network has to be shared, or for efficiency should be shared, on a basis which opens up markets at either end to competition.

My distinction between pure and rivalrous common carriage then rests on the extent to which the operator of the common facility can also participate in providing other services, for example, buying gas and distributing it to final consumers or providing rival long-distance telephone service, as well as transmitting it down the pipeline or operating a local loop. If the common carrier is excluded from such activities, then it should be immune from the temptation to run the common carriage business in a way which sustains its operations in other markets. If it is involved in other markets, so that the common carriage is rivalrous, then incentives inevitably become muddied.

Even pure common carriage has its difficulties. Because it is, by assumption, a monopoly, the operator has to be regulated in some way. This may take the form of cost plus (rate of return) regulation or of a price cap. The latter probably has more favourable incentive properties, although - as many commentators have pointed out - the distinction between the two may not be clear-cut. Then there is the question of relative prices within an overall revenue total. Since the network may be a complex one, with local capacity constraints, alternative routing available, and so on, setting those relative prices in an efficient way is a very complex process.

The closest to an example of pure common carriage in the United Kingdom is the National Grid Company. Even here, because the Grid is owned by the regional electricity companies, restrictions are placed on the owners' capacity to interfere in policy-making. But the current review of National Grid Company prices, which I am confident many of the audience know far more about than I do, demonstrates that finding an efficient set of prices which yield proper incentives to invest is a complex business. (What we are concerned about - please note - is incentives not only for efficient investment by generation, but also by the Grid itself.) It is also true that customers of the system are not backward in lobbying the regulator in pursuit of their own preferred charging patterns. But at least the accounting arrangements and incentives for the common carrier are fully segregated from those of its customers.

In what I call rivalrous common carriage, the network owner both provides transmission services to other companies and competes with them for custom in other markets. This system characterises both the gas industry, where under the agreement recently reached between the Office of Fair Trading and British Gas Corporation up to 60 per cent of gas transmitted through BGC's network for the industrial market will be owned by other suppliers, and the telecommunications industry, where BT both provides interconnect or wholesale services to other operators such as Mercury, and competes with them across a broad range of markets.

It is here that the incentives to use ownership of the common carrier as an anti-competitive weapon become most severe. By overcharging for the common carrier provided, the incumbent can keep out what would be an efficient entrant. Moreover, unless prohibited from doing so, it can price discriminate to protect its vulnerable markets. Its market power can be further enhanced by delays in providing interconnection and by the provision of low-quality service. Any or all of these methods or the fear of them may be enough to thwart the ambitions of a potentially efficient entrant.

One way of preventing this, now tried under the gas settlement, is to impose accounting separation on the common carriage element, with a requirement that its owner must charge its associated companies the same amount for the transmission of their gas as it charges rival firms. Any raising of charges to profit from or deter rivals will then be reflected in excessive returns - if they can be proven. This is all very well provided that the rules for accounting separation are watertight enough. If not, some deterrence may be achieved.

This still leaves open the principles on which transmission or conveyance charges should be set. Sir James McKinnon argues that this should be left as much as possible to the parties concerned, with the regulator acting as referee in a minimum number of cases. But because the interests of the two sides are so diametrically opposed, it is unlikely that agreement will easily be reached. Indeed, in the telecommunications industry virtually all interconnection agreements have had to be determined by the Director-General.

When interconnection charges have been set by the regulator, two obvious principles for setting them suggest themselves. The first is fully allocated costs and the second is incremental costs. Interconnection determinations in telecommunications have been guided since 1984 by an ingenious compromise or half-way house between these alternatives: 'fully allocated costs attributable to the services to be provided and taking into account relevant overheads and a reasonable rate of return on attributable assets'. Other regulated industries have different formulae. That in the gas industry has, I believe, been controversial.

This approach has, however, recently come under attack from the distinguished American economist, William Baumol. He illustrates his alternative approach by taking an example from the railway industry (where, too, interconnection may become a feature in the United Kingdom if the Conservative Government is returned). The proposition is illustrated in the following example. A journey from A to C consists of two segments, A to B and B to C. The incumbent can supply each segment at an incremental cost of £3 and provision of the route overall yields a contribution of £4 to overheads. The total cost of the journey from A to C is thus £10. Suppose an entrant comes in who only offers services from A to B but for some reason has to buy component B to C from the incumbent. The question for the regulator is how much the entrant can be required to pay for access to the component from B to C. The perhaps surprising answer is that the efficient component price (in terms of promoting entry) is neither the incremental cost of £3 nor the full allocated cost of £5 but the incremental cost of B to C plus the opportunity cost to the incumbent, its contribution to overheads of £4. This is desirable, because it yields an efficient entry signal. A charge of £3 or even £5 for the segment from B to C would encourage an entrant to enter the competitive stretch from A to B even if its incremental costs were well above those of the incumbent. This is another application of the Baumol principle of constrained market pricing, where prices can be set at will between incremental and stand-alone cost.

The obvious danger in applying this principle is that if the incumbent is inefficient in providing the component which it sells to others, or is inefficient elsewhere in its business, the contribution it earns on its monopoly segment will be exaggerated, and application of the rule will cause entrants to bear the burden of the entrant's inefficiency. The correct principle is that interconnection charges should be paid at incremental cost plus contribution, where both of these are based upon the data of an efficient operator; but this is clearly difficult for a regulator to implement if he or she has only one (possibly inefficient) observation. It is also a purely static argument and ignores the galvanising effect of entry on the time-path of costs.

My conclusions, therefore, are that common carriage or interconnection is a major weapon in the regulator's armoury, and an extremely important route to competition. It is also, as Sir James argues, quite practicable: UK regulators have supervised its operation in gas, electricity and telecommunications, and there are obvious lessons from this for the rest of Europe. At the same time, regulating interconnection is by no means an easy process.

Gas is both storable and - up to a point - homogeneous. This makes it easier to set common carriage rates. In other industries where neither or only one of these conditions applies, the problem is more complex, but equally important for the development of competition.

3

UTILITY REGULATION AND THE MONOPOLIES AND MERGERS COMMISSION: RETROSPECT AND PROSPECT

Sir Sydney Lipworth

Chairman, Monopolies and Mergers Commission

Introduction

IT IS GENERALLY ACCEPTED WISDOM that monopolies need watching. The temptation, so the argument goes, is for organisations in monopoly positions, whether in the public or private sector, to exploit their dominant position for their own benefit. In the absence of the checks and balances provided by market forces, prices would be higher, choice reduced and quality of service lower than in a competitive environment. To counter this the Director General of Fair Trading (DGFT), since 1973 (and the DTI before him), has been keeping a constant eye on British industry as a whole, examining the activities of major companies, looking at specific markets and evaluating allegations of monopoly abuse.

As the utilities have been privatised - and from the Monopolies and Mergers Commission (MMC) point of view this includes airports as well as telecommunications, gas, electricity and water - taking their monopoly, or near-monopoly, position into the private sector, each has had a specific regulator appointed to monitor its activities. These regulators, the Civil Aviation Authority and the Directors General of Telecommunications, Gas Supply, Electricity Supply and Water Services, have all been appointed since 1984.

These monitoring activities are complemented by the rôle of the MMC. Its functions and objectives are, however, very different from those of the regulators and the DGFT. In this talk I shall be considering the change in the regulatory régime and the potential consequences for the utilities as they have moved from being monopolies in the public sector to monopolies in the private sector. But first, a word or two about the MMC and its developing rôle in monopoly and competition control.

The Development of the MMC

The MMC has been involved in monopoly regulation since 1948 when it was established as the Monopolies and Restrictive Practices Commission. Until then the UK had no formal competition policy; matters, including abuse of monopoly positions, were left largely to the common law on conspiracy and contracts in restraint of trade. The Monopolies and Restrictive Practices (Inquiry and Control) Act 1948 dealt with monopolies in the supply of goods and restrictive trade practices and agreements, although neither monopolies nor restrictive trade practices or agreements were made illegal *per se*. There was only to be intervention in the market and action on them if they were found, on a full and independent investigation, to be operating against the public interest.

The rôle of the then Monopolies and Restrictive Practices Commission was to investigate these conditions on a reference made to it by the President of the Board of Trade to whom it would report on the public interest effects.The Minister was empowered to take the relevant action to remedy any adverse effect identified by the Commission.

Seven years later, in 1956, the responsibility for *restrictive trade practices* was hived off, leaving the Monopolies Commission with the investigation of monopoly situations in the supply of goods and certain general references of industry-wide practices. In 1965, following a wave of mergers, investigations into *mergers*, including *newspaper mergers*, were introduced to the Commission. The same Act also extended the monopoly provisions to include the supply of *services*. The Fair Trading Act (FTA) then came along in 1973 consolidating the Commission's work, and introducing the title, *Monopolies and Mergers Commission*. It also added references concerned with certain *labour practices* and established the position and rôle of the Director General of Fair Trading.

In 1980 the Competition Act empowered the DGFT to refer to the

MMC a new type of work, anti-competitive practices of *individual firms* (even if not enjoying monopoly power). It also introduced a new class of work to the MMC - investigation of the efficiency of public sector bodies, including the utilities. Since then the five privatisation statutes - the Telecommunications Act 1984; the Airports and Gas Acts of 1986; and the Water and Electricity Acts of 1989 (in the case of water, the relevant provisions are now in the Water Industry Act 1991) - have added a further variety of work which I shall deal with later in more detail.

Many people still overlook the nationalised and privatised industry aspect of the MMC's work. Our title of course invites a concentration on the monopolies and mergers aspects of our workload. And this is still the major part of our activities, monopolies accounting for the longest and most in-depth inquiries and mergers the greatest, in terms of numbers. But even the broad merger classification hides the special provisions relating to the MMC's involvement in newspaper mergers, and also now mergers of water undertakings.

As my survey of the MMC's developing rôle has shown, the work of the MMC straddles most areas of UK industrial and economic life, most industries and most economic activities. We now also receive references from a number of different sources: the Secretary of State for Trade and Industry, the Director General of Fair Trading, the Civil Aviation Authority and the Directors General who regulate the other utilities.

Independence

But, whatever the source or nature of the reference, the MMC has not been involved in, and remains independent of, reference policy or in the decision to refer an individual case. Nor, even if it were to make recommendations for action in a report, is it involved in the enforcement of action following the report. This distinguishes the rôle of the MMC from other regulatory agencies. The MMC is thus free from any internal conflicts of interest that may be generated by the decision to proceed or by a recommendation to adopt a particular 'remedy'. There is, therefore, separation of powers.

An, if not the, essential feature of the MMC is its independence from the bodies deciding upon a reference and to whom a report has to be submitted. The MMC has no view on whether or not a particular reference should be made. It does, however, carry out its investigation thoroughly

41

and fairly and free from any conflicts of interest or extraneous pressure. I believe this independence, and the publication of the full inquiry report, are important if the MMC is to be able, and also to be seen, to carry out its task fairly and without prejudice. But whatever the nature of the inquiry, the purpose of the MMC is constant: to provide an independent investigation into matters of public interest.

As an independent body the MMC has control over its own procedures, the foundation of which is fairness. Anyone has the opportunity to present evidence to MMC inquiries and to raise issues for consideration. The procedures are sufficiently flexible to cater for all contingencies without disadvantage to a party to an inquiry or a person presenting evidence. There is recognition of the importance to main parties of being informed of the relevant issues and arguments. All this with the concern for confidentiality of what is often commercially sensitive information.

Section 11, Competition Act 1980

Before 1980 public sector bodies, such as utilities, were in general outside the competition law, and hence outside the remit of the MMC. Then in 1980, the utilities were among the public sector bodies specifically brought within the remit of the MMC under Section 11 of the 1980 Competition Act. This empowered the Secretary of State to refer to the MMC any question relating to (i) the efficiency and costs of, and (ii) the service provided by, nationalised industries and certain other public sector bodies such as, for example, the water and electricity boards, the Post Office, British Rail, or (iii) any possible abuse by them of a monopoly situation. The rationale was that they were monopolies and hence not subject to competitive forces. As a surrogate for competition the MMC was to examine the service they provided to ensure they gave value for money. With very few exceptions such bodies were not then accountable, as is a plc, to shareholders.

In fact, independent audits of the efficiency of public sector utilities began in this country in 1968. In that year the National Board for Prices and Incomes (NBPI) was strengthened specifically for the purpose of inquiring into the efficiency of all industries whose proposals for price increases were referred to it. The MMC first came into the picture as early as 1970 with the proposal to amalgamate the NBPI and the MMC in a 'Commission for Industry and Manpower'. Increased efficiency was specifically mentioned as something to be considered by the Commission.

The Bill fell with the change of government in 1970, but in 1977 a new Act gave the Price Commission the discretion to investigate most price increases by nationalised industries and their efficiency as well. The Price Commission was abolished by the Competition Act 1980 and the same Act conferred on the MMC the powers to audit the efficiency of nationalised industries. The government of the day said that it had concluded that the MMC was the most suitable body.

The range of matters that could be covered in an efficiency audit under Section 11 of the 1980 Act was limited. Basically the MMC investigation was confined (and the actual reference might narrow this further) to questions relating to the body's efficiency and costs, quality of service and any abuse of monopoly power. The recommendations by the MMC relate to the matters falling within the reference, and in practice the MMC is not concerned with wider remedies such as price controls, divestment and structural changes.

The public sector bodies are answerable to their sponsoring Minister and his department. References, although made normally by the Secretary of State for Trade and Industry, in practice required the sponsoring Minister's consent, and any recommendations, if based on an adverse finding against the public interest, could be modified or overridden by the Secretary of State.

This has changed where privatisation has taken place. Instead of being monitored generally by a sponsoring department, the utilities now have a specialist regulator, whose ongoing function (indeed *raison d'être*) includes inducing them to keep costs and prices down, improve efficiency, maintain appropriate levels of investment and introduce competition.

Privatisation

In general, privatisation represented an attempt to remove political influence - though not necessarily immediately (for example, golden shares) and/or wholly - and a move towards competitive disciplines that would encourage cost and management structures (and cultures) that were commercially and market orientated. The majority of privatisations were of businesses which faced strong competition, particularly international competition (oil, steel, cars, airlines), and the competition authorities' normal rôle applied, including that of the MMC, without any specialist regulator.

The utilities represented an exceptional case. Some viewed their public ownership as a necessary response to possible or perceived market failures. In many cases the argument for regulation was not necessarily applicable to the whole business of a utility industry and competitive forces were strong in some markets in which undertakings operated. In some instances there were choices about the form of the privatisation which would have allowed more competitive structures (for example, selling power stations in smaller groups), though that may not have generated similar revenue benefits from privatisation.

Regulation was not necessarily designed to be a long-term replacement for the competitive market. A primary aim of the regulatory régimes was to introduce competition and maximise the extent to which normal competitive forces would be sufficient and thus avoid the need for further involvement.

The nature of regulation, its principles, scope and direction and, at least initially, the powers of the regulator, were not identical. Each of the industries is very different and its regulation needs to reflect that. The nature of competition, including its absence, varied from industry to industry. And the privatisation exercise was extended over a broadly five-year period during which expectations changed and lessons were learnt.

Privatisation Reference Provisions

Turning now to privatisation legislation, the MMC has statutory functions (or functions which assist regulation) under the five privatisation statutes. Each of these Acts provides for an individual or body with specific functions in the regulation of the industry concerned. With one exception (the Civil Aviation Authority), these regulators have been specifically created. They, like the DGFT, have a continuous function, the MMC only an occasional one. However, while the statutory functions of the MMC under (principally) the FTA in relation to the industry as a whole apply in general to the utilities as well, the privatisation legislation provides additional functions for the MMC in relation to specific utilities which go beyond the Fair Trading Act provisions.

Reference to the MMC by the regulators under the five Acts divide, broadly, into three. The *first* is - with variations - common to all. It arises when a decision by the regulator to modify a condition (or conditions) of the licence (to use a comprehensive expression - for example, under the

Water Act it is an 'appointment') governing the operation of that industry is disputed by the licence holder. In that event, the regulator's only recourse is to make a reference, in essence asking the MMC to investigate whether the matter specified in the reference operates against the public interest, and if so whether a licence modification is an appropriate remedy. The finding on the public interest has to be accepted by the regulator. Recommendations as to licence modifications to meet adverse effects identified by the MMC in its Report are then taken into account by the regulator in reaching a final view, but he need not adopt those made by the MMC.

The only instance so far of such a licence modification reference concerned Chatline and Message Services under the Telecommunications Act.

The *second* occasion for references applies, as mentioned earlier, only to the Airports and Water Acts. The Airports Act provides for a special treatment of airport charges of 'designated airports' (Heathrow, Gatwick and Stansted, and Manchester airports) involving a five-yearly review of their charges and a mandatory reference to the MMC, and additionally requires investigation of whether there has been a course of conduct operating against the public interest in respect of, for example, commercial rents. Again, the MMC's recommendations (including those on charging) are taken into account by the CAA in reaching its decision.

An analogous procedure has been created in the case of the water industry, although this has not yet been invoked. This procedure requires the Director General of Water Services (DGWS) to undertake five- or 10-yearly periodic reviews of charges - with a provision for more limited interim reviews if requested by the water undertakings. However, and putting it very briefly, in the event of a dispute between an undertaker and the DGWS on these matters, the DGWS is required to make a reference to the MMC. The MMC's subsequent findings must be implemented rather than just taken into consideration.

The two are thus similar in that the reference to the MMC is mandatory. In the case of water the MMC's determination is final. In the case of the airports, the MMC's finding is not, and the CAA, itself a public sector body with a range of activities as well as being a regulator, has the final say. The question has been raised whether, if a reference to an independent body like the MMC is mandatory, the MMC's decision should not be final as in water.

The *third* circumstance in which a reference of a privatised industry arises relates specifically to water and is the requirement upon the Secretary of State to refer any merger of water enterprises meeting certain criteria. The Water Act also specified a public interest test unique to this type of inquiry including a requirement, subsequently simplified in the Utilities Act (the concept of 'water enterprises under independent control' has been removed), to have regard to the principle that the number of water enterprises should not be reduced so as to prejudice the DGWS's ability to make a comparison between different such enterprises.

Effect of Transition to the Private Sector

Viewed from the vantage point of the MMC and its rôle in relation to the privatised utilities, a major effect of their transition from the public to the private sector is that they have emerged from Section 11 efficiency references to a much more rigorous regulatory régime. Efficiency audit references exposed their operations - costs and efficiency, service, etc. - to MMC scrutiny and investigation. The MMC, as an impartial examiner, would identify areas that required improvement and make recommendations for change, which were generally accepted, and indeed often welcomed. But their structure would not be potentially threatened by this.

Now, on the one side, they have a specialised regulator (where previously they had a sponsoring department), who is pro-active, initiating inquiries, seeking information, setting conditions of operation, introducing licence modifications, limiting charges, etc. If they do not agree (or in the case of airports, every five years), there is a reference to the MMC under the specific legislation. On the other side, not only is their regulator seeking to increase competition in their industry, but they are also exposed to all the general competition legislation; the additional involvement of the Director General of Fair Trading and the prospect of references under the Fair Trading Act (monopoly references and references of general practices in the industry) and the Competition Act (anti-competitive practices of individual firms).[1]

[1] Under the Competition Act 1980, references of anti-competitive practices of public sector bodies could be referred to the MMC, e.g. London Electricity Board in 1982 and Highland Scottish Omnibus Ltd in 1989, but these were rare. The DGFT could also be asked to report on prices.

The potential consequences of adverse findings by the MMC under the general competition legislation can be far-reaching: for example, price controls; divestment or division of businesses; disposal of shareholdings; restructuring of the industry, publication of prices and other information; declaring the making or carrying out of agreements unlawful and prohibiting any tie-in of the supply of certain goods and services to other action by the customer; prohibiting courses of conduct. However, the one constant is the MMC, with its very important characteristics of being totally neutral and unbiased and completely independent of government, the regulated or the regulators, as well as the fact that each investigation is determined on its own facts and circumstances without *a priori* views or presumptions.

The important point is that, even if the consequences of an MMC investigation under the privatisation or the competition legislation could potentially be far-reaching (and perhaps more so than under the efficiency audit references), there are important safeguards:

(1) There can be no such adverse consequences unless the MMC, after a thorough and fair inquiry, has found that there are matters operating against the public interest that require these remedies;

(2) If the MMC finds that the matters in question do not operate against the public interest that decision is final;

(3) In the case of adverse findings and recommendations under the general legislation the Secretary of State still has an overriding discretion to modify or even reject (seldom done) adverse findings or recommendations;

(4) In the privatisation legislation, apart from water charges determinations where the MMC's decision is final, the regulators can modify the MMC's findings, but must take them into account.

All of this means that the utility, if it does not agree with the proposals of the regulator or the DGFT, cannot be compelled to do so unless there has been a full MMC inquiry and adverse findings.

Subject to what I have said about finality, the MMC's rôle is therefore very much as an adjudicator between the regulator and the utility in the

47

event of dispute. With the exception of automatic references relating to airport charges and certain water company mergers, references are made only when the sides directly involved cannot resolve a dispute between them.

The Utilities

I want now to turn briefly to consider the MMC's involvement with each of the utilities.

Water

Since 1980 there have been five efficiency audits and three post-privatisation merger inquiries into the water industry. Directly and indirectly, recommendations from a number of efficiency audit reports have been significant for developments in this industry. One of the first of these was the recommendation in the 1981 report on the inquiry into the Severn Trent Water Authority and the Waterworks companies of East Worcester and South Staffordshire that the boards of water authorities should not be based predominantly on local authority representatives.

Another aspect of the efficiency audit inquiries has been the assessment of the comparative efficiency of companies in the industry. The 1986 inquiry into the Southern Water Authority (SWA) and the six companies operating in its area compared the efficiency of the seven bodies in terms of trends in their performance as measured by 13 performance indicators. These included various cost factors expressed per head of population, per property supplied or per megalitre of water supplied. The MMC recommended that the SWA should develop its performance indicators further as the basis for setting quantified targets. This inquiry also took the analysis of comparative performance indicators a stage further. Data from a total of 28 companies were used as the basis for a systematic regression analysis. This showed that it was possible to explain over 90 per cent of the variation between companies in both manpower costs and materials costs in terms of linear relationships with the number of properties supplied. This work ultimately led to the setting of RPI-K targets for the industry, a formula devised to maintain a balance between the need to ensure that water companies can finance their activities and the interests of consumers in relation to charges and annual price increases.

It was also in the report on this inquiry that the MMC made clear its view that, while the issue of privatising the water industry was not within its remit, the existing private statutory companies were not in its view a useful model to follow. Where private concerns had monopoly power over essential services, the need was to combine adequate safeguards for the consumer with some appropriate means of providing a profit incentive to management to reduce costs and increase efficiency. The form of regulation - that is, by limiting profits and dividends - then applied to the statutory companies failed to meet this need.

Looking to possible future MMC involvement, the DGWS has given notice of a periodic price review in 1994 for implementation of charges from 1 April 1995, five years after the introduction of the new system. If all of the undertakings were to dispute their determinations this could mean the MMC being faced with 33 references at one time. Additionally, requests from the undertakings at any time for interim determinations could lead to references, as might licence modifications arising from EC directives.

Electricity

Electricity has been subject to MMC investigation more frequently than any of the other utilities, with the possible exception of the water industry. Together with gas it featured in the first investigation by the MMC into the utilities. This was a general reference in 1971 when the then Monopolies Commission investigated the principles governing the level and character of connection charges for electricity and gas and whether practice met those principles. The gas industry received a clean bill of health but some action was recommended to bring the electricity industry into line.

Then, between 1980 and the 1989 Electricity Act, the MMC conducted eight Competition Act inquiries into the industry, seven of them efficiency audits. These covered a wide range of activities in the industry: through the CEGB's generation and transmission of electricity in bulk, the efficiency and costs of various Area Electricity Boards, and the domestic electrical goods retailing activities of the London Electricity Board. The last was not an efficiency audit but an anti-competitive practice inquiry concerned with the LEB's practice of maintaining price competitiveness by financing losses on appliance retailing out of profits from electricity supply.

49

The report on the first of the CEGB efficiency audits again reflected the politically sensitive position of the utilities. This concluded that the Board, in respect of its purchasing policies, could have had lower costs. Aspects of this were the fact that at times the Board was prevented from importing coal at prices lower than those of the NCB; that it was required to pursue a 'Buy British' policy in procurement of plant; and the Government having twice ordered a power station 'in advance of need' which led to those power stations being unusually expensive. No adverse finding was recorded in respect of the public interest arising from this but the observations again reflect the non-commercial factors inherent in the operations of the public sector utilities.

As with water, the examination and development of performance indicators has been a common feature of several efficiency audit inquiries into the electricity industry. In the 1981 CEGB inquiry the MMC recommended that the Board should further develop the use of its power station operating performance indicator to provide additional information to management, both at the individual power stations and in the centre. Both the Yorkshire Electricity Board report in 1983 and the South Wales Electricity Board report in 1984 included an analysis of each board's performance compared with the rest of the industry, based on numerous performance indicators. The YEB report recommended that the board should be more selective in its use of performance indicators and set a small number of more challenging targets relating to its key objectives. The SWALEB report recommended that the Board should make more use of quantified medium-term targets, particularly for cost reduction and for manpower.

The 1985 inquiry into the revenue collection system of four area electricity boards compared the boards' performance in terms of numerous efficiency indicators. The MMC found an unsatisfactory variation in the types of performance indicator in use and recommended use of the same key performance measures for revenue collection which would then form the basis for best practice in revenue collection in the industry.

Future electricity references might conceivably arise out of the new licence condition on National Power and Powergen proposed in the OFFER consultation document issued at the end of last year and arising out of its pool price inquiry and relating to the availability of plant and the closure or mothballing of generating stations. And, as OFFER said in its

Annual Report, work has now started on the National Grid Company's transmission charges price control which is due for replacement on 1 April 1993.

Airports

The MMC first had involvement with airports in 1985, the year before the privatisation legislation was enacted, when it undertook an efficiency audit into the British Airports Authority and the seven airports operated by it, concluding that while there were areas in which BAA should improve its operations (for example, some aspects of quality of service to customers, competition in service to airlines, encouraging greater competition in sales to the public, competition in the supply of aircraft fuel), these did not operate against the public interest. BAA has been investigated again since privatisation under the provision for mandatory five-year price reviews by the MMC, though this applies only to its South East airports operations at Heathrow, Gatwick and Stansted. The other airport designated for these five-year reviews is Manchester which was referred to us in 1987 and 1991. The second inquiry is still proceeding: it is due to report to the CAA in early June this year with the next quinquennial review not then due until BAA comes to us again in 1995.

In its first report on Manchester Airport, the Commission recommended that airports charges should increase by no more than RPI-1, a similar requirement to that imposed by the Secretary of State on the BAA airports for the first five years after privatisation. This recommendation was broadly accepted by the CAA, although they adopted a slightly different form of regulation. No course of conduct by Manchester Airport was found to be against the public interest.

In the BAA report last year, the Commission proposed that prices should increase by no more than RPI-4, although we also recommended that this be relaxed as and when BAA started the construction of Terminal 5 at Heathrow. The CAA initially proposed a much tougher formula, of RPI-8, but finally compromised between their proposal and our recommendation (with a formula varying over the quinquennium - RPI-8 in the first two years, RPI-4 in the third and RPI-1 in the last two). The Commission also found one aspect of BAA's course of conduct to be against the public interest. The Airports Act excludes from the formal scope of price regulation a wide range of services necessary for the airlines to operate at the airport: for example, rentals on check-in desks.

51

The MMC concluded that it was against the public interest for charges to be levied without user airlines being given the information on the costs associated with each of these activities and recommended (and the CAA accepted) that this information should be provided. Airports also featured in the British Airways/Sabena merger inquiry in 1990 when the question of slot allocation at United Kingdom airports was one of the issues addressed.

Telecommunications

The MMC has had no involvement in this sector by way of monopoly inquiries or efficiency audits. Inquiries to date have been one proposed merger and the Chatline and Message Services inquiries, both post-privatisation. In addition, the industry has of course been subject to a pricing and duopoly review by the Secretary of State for Trade and Industry.

As I have said, the Chatline and Message Services inquiry was under the privatisation legislation and concerned the provision of these services over the BT network. It was important more for its being the first (to date only) licence modification inquiry undertaken under the privatisation legislation than for the significance of the matter under inquiry, though the subject was of course of great concern to many customers. In making the reference the DG for Telecommunications did not specify a proposed licence modification but asked for consideration to be given to three possible changes. In the event, the MMC recommended a modification stronger than those put forward, based on the principle of giving customers full control over the use made of telephones.

The merger was the potentially very significant proposal by British Telecommunications to acquire a controlling interest in the telecommunications equipment manufacturer Mitel Corporation. The MMC concluded that the merger would have adverse effects on competition between both manufacturers and distributors of telecommunications equipment, being likely, *inter alia*, to operate seriously to reduce the growth of competition in the market with adverse effects on telecommunications users through reduced choice and higher prices. To remedy this, the MMC recommended that BT be prevented from acquiring for its use in its public network or for supply in the UK telecommunications apparatus produced by Mitel; subject to this the merger could proceed.

To prevent a company from using and distributing its subsidiary's products is unusual. But BT had been allowed as a privately-owned company to retain much of the monopoly power its predecessors enjoyed as a public corporation. In the MMC's view, competition in the home market, one of the principal objects of the transfer of BT to the private sector the year before, could be safeguarded by BT's acceptance of the recommendations and that this would not prejudice its wish to achieve a place in the international market.

As everyone knows OFTEL is currently in the midst of its first price regulation review which may possibly yield a reference over the coming weeks.

Gas

Gas is so far the odd one out of the utilities, not having been considered previously by the MMC by way of an efficiency audit or under privatisation legislation. It has not escaped attention, however. In addition to the 1971 monopoly inquiry into electricity and gas connection, between 1977 and 1980 a monopoly inquiry was carried out into the supply of domestic gas appliances in the UK. The report on this inquiry demonstrated how politically sensitive the position of the utilities has always been. Having concluded that British Gas was operating in this area in a way contrary to the public interest, the MMC put forward two options to remedy the position. The first was that British Gas should discontinue its retailing function. The second was that British Gas should receive some precise directives for the allocation of costs in publishing separate accounts for its appliance retailing and installation and contracting services. The majority report, however, expressed no preference between these options, commenting instead that

'We recognise that, when Ministers decide what course to adopt in relation to the BGC, they may have to take into consideration not only the matters which we have discussed, but also political considerations upon which the Commission does not normally form a view'.

Since privatisation the MMC has undertaken a major monopoly inquiry under the terms of the Fair Trading Act, the 1988 report and the supply of gas by British Gas to contract customers. This inquiry found extensive discrimination by British Gas in the pricing and supply of gas to contract customers attributable to the existence of a monopoly situation.

The inquiry report recommendations were directed towards encouraging competition in the supply of gas by restraining discriminatory pricing and supply by British Gas until competition was effective. In particular, it was recommended that in order to encourage the emergence of new gas suppliers, British Gas should not initially contract for more than 90 per cent of deliveries from any new gas field within the UK continental shelf.

Thus began a process to increase competition in the supply of gas to industrial and commercial users. Indeed, at the beginning of last month (March 1992) new undertakings were given to the DGFT by British Gas which will lead to its share of the contract gas market reducing to 40 per cent by 1995, thereby increasing the potential for competition and improved service to customers in the contract gas market. As I am sure most of you will recall, the alternative to these new undertakings by British Gas was reportedly a further reference to the MMC.

British Gas and the possibility of it being subject to, or seeking, a reference to the MMC in respect of different aspects of its business have of course been in the news of late. We have, however, yet to be involved.

Prospect

That then is broadly where the MMC and the utilities stand in relation to each other today, and how experience has been gained and the relationship has developed in reaching today's position. I now want to consider the 'prospect', and to do this by posing a number of questions that arise out of experience so far of the privatised utilities, their relationship with their respective regulators, and the rôle of the MMC in their regulation.

(a) Frequency of MMC Involvement

First, is the still only occasional MMC input sufficient? Does it, should it, answer the question: *Quis custodiet ipsos custodes?* Should the MMC spotlight be focussed more frequently on the industry as a whole in order to make the process of regulation more transparent? The regulator has a number of balances to strike, yet its dealings with its industry and the reasoning behind its decisions lack transparency. An MMC inquiry, on the other hand, is carried out by an independent body and summaries of evidence presented to the inquiry and detailed reasons for the conclusions reached are published in its reports.

While there is a tension between the regulator and its utility, the close contact between the two over time will inevitably increase familiarity and perhaps erode the authority of the regulator. Specialist knowledge for the regulator is important if it is to fulfil its function but it should not be dependent on the industry for maintaining this. Would more frequent MMC involvement guard against 'regulator capture' or at any rate demonstrate that there has not been 'regulator capture'?

(b) MMC as the Final Arbiter

Secondly, should the MMC's rôle be more determinative? While MMC reports and recommendations following reference inquiries under the privatisation legislation are fully taken into account by the relevant regulator in reaching a final decision, in only one instance, that of price determination for the water, and water and sewerage, undertakings, is the MMC conclusion final.[2] Would it be more desirable for the regulator to have discretion in respect of price determination references but for the MMC conclusions to be final?

(c) 'Super-Regulator'

Thirdly, what should be the long-term approach to the utilities? The regulatory régimes have already been subject to change since their introduction and future development is inevitable. It is high on the agenda of all political parties. It has already been suggested in a number of quarters that in time individual regulators would be unnecessary and that a single regulatory organisation would be established. This may help in avoiding regulatory capture but could face the presentational difficulty of having to adopt different policies and courses of action in respect of the different utilities because of their respective characteristics. This would create an even greater concern if lack of transparency in negotiation and decision-making prevail. It might be thought that a development on these lines could lead to more frequent involvement of the MMC to help ensure consistency of treatment as between industries.

(d) Price Control vs. Competition

Fourthly, must the conflict between price control and competition be seen as everlasting? One of the challenges the regulators face is striking the

---

2. Except, of course, where the MMC finds that the matter in question does not operate against the public interest, in which case the finding is final.

balance between controlling the prices of the utilities and encouraging competition. Increasing emphasis is placed upon controlling prices for the benefit of consumers. But if competition is to be increased the market-place has to be sufficiently attractive to encourage new entrants. Low profitability may not achieve this.

Balance is called for in the relationship between consumers of and shareholders in the privatised utilities. Many shareholders in the utilities are new to the stock market. While they may have read the warnings that the value of their shares can fall as well as increase there is inevitably a belief among some that the Government will protect their investment. But for a return on that investment the company must earn sufficient profits to pay reasonable dividends. Are those profits to be earned at the expense of high prices to consumers - even though this may bring in competition? Are dividends to be paid at the cost of investment in the business to improve services? The utilities face huge requirements for capital investment. Reasonable profits and reasonable certainty and stability in the industry are necessary to keep costs of capital down or even ensure a reasonable availability of capital funding. While all utilities may in time have to produce separate reports and accounts for their regulated and non-regulated businesses, how can consumers be sure that acquisitions are not being financed by the utilities' business? Or, conversely, can shareholders be confident that the diversified businesses are not being required to subsidise the utilities' activities?

There seems to be an inherent conflict of interest between the objectives of the regulator and the regulated, or at least there will be conflicts at different times. These inherent conflicts of interest may result in a greater MMC rôle.

(e) RPI-X

Fifthly, is the RPI-X formula the most appropriate form of price regulation? In the BAA case there was argument from some quarters for a change from RPI-X. That is, prices of the regulated operators are only allowed to rise by the rate of inflation less an 'X' factor set for a period of time, usually five years. Broadly, this formula has been adopted in the UK to provide a greater incentive on a firm to reduce costs. Over the long term it can be regarded as relating prices to costs, as well as a means of providing an incentive to reduce costs and improve efficiency, thereby enabling the regulated company to reap benefits achieved through improved profitability. Among the alternatives is regulation on the basis of rate of return. Although more directly based on costs, the argument against it was that it either allowed increases in operating or capital costs to be passed on to the user with little incentive to control such costs, or it required continual regulatory scrutiny of the cost base. The MMC preferred the RPI-X formula because of the incentive it gave to the regulated firm to behave efficiently. It is also the effective formula that it has recommended in a number of private sector monopoly inquiries, for example, White Salt, Breakfast Cereals and, most recently, Matches.

Conclusion

It would be an exceptional achievement if all of the regulators were able to strike all of these balances to the satisfaction of everyone - a mission impossible perhaps. Disputes are bound to arise, and while, as I said earlier, most will be resolved between the two sides, the potential for more frequent MMC involvement increases with each expansion of the rôle of the regulators.

But one basic question which in time will need to be considered is whether the public utility monopolies do need separate specialist watchdogs. The long-term intention is that they should become industries operating to all intents and purposes in the same way as any other industry. In these circumstances, is it not appropriate that they should be dealt with in the same way, that is subject to monitoring by the DGFT, with references to the MMC? These references could be either under the general competition legislation or, if appropriate, under specialist legislation applying to the particular industry. Whatever the answers to the questions I have posed, it seems to be inevitable that the MMC and the utilities will have a long-term relationship with each other.

UTILITY REGULATION AND THE MONOPOLIES AND MERGERS COMMISSION: RETROSPECT AND PROSPECT

DISCUSSANT:
Professor John Kay

London Economics

The unfinished business of privatisation will be a major part of the political agenda for the 1990s. I think it is certain that the MMC will have a substantial rôle to play in setting that agenda and in influencing its outcome, and this is the subject on which Sir Sydney Lipworth has so effectively focussed our attention this evening.

Let me begin by spelling out why the privatisation agenda is indeed unfinished. First, privatisation, and the regulation associated with it, was an experiment and it is an experiment from which we have learnt. One need only trace through the evolution of the great utility privatisations - from telecoms through gas and water to electricity - to see that learning process in operation. Second, it is a process that was accompanied by a good deal of naïvety. In particular, it was often believed that, once transferred to the private sector, the major utilities could simply become commercial businesses like any other. This view was held both by government and by the managers of the firms themselves. It is one which is true of some of the businesses that were in the public sector in 1980 but, as events have shown, it is not true of most of them.

The third reason why the agenda is unfinished is that the period after privatisation is one in which there is a marked shift in the bargaining power of the principal parties to the issues. Incumbent management never has so much power as it does in the days immediately before shares are offered to the public. Once flotation has occurred, monopoly utilities are not popular and their battles with their regulators have not been successful ones. In telecoms the X in RPI-X formula has risen from 3 to $6^1/4$. There have been similar developments in gas, in airports, and it is clear that the direction of change in the water industry is similar.

Our subject tonight - the rôle of the Monopolies and Mergers Commission in utility regulation - raises one basic question immediately. Is it right that the Monopolies and Mergers Commission should have the power which the various Acts give it as, in effect, the arbiter in event of dispute between the regulator and the utility. If there has to be some appeal in the face of such disagreement - and it is clear that there does have to be some such method of appeal - there are only two alternatives to the MMC: the Courts and the Secretary of State. The weakness of the Courts is that they lack the investigative powers and capabilities which a Commission investigation can generate. And the objections are even more obvious if the Secretary of State is the court of appeal. It would then be certain that the doors of the Secretary of State would be constantly opening and shutting in the face of industry lobbying in a manner which would be bound to undermine the whole structure of arm's length regulation.

But so far the Monopolies and Mergers Commission has been the dog that has not barked. It has played a rôle in those industries - airports - where its intervention is required by statute, but not where its intervention depends on the parties choosing to seek its aid. The only case so far, as Sir Sydney noted, has been that of Chatlines. And the explanation of this absence of references is that utilities have backed off in the face of the prospect of an MMC reference. Sir Sydney has emphasised the transparency of his procedures. In the main, regulator and regulatee have preferred to do a deal behind the scenes than to have their affairs trawled over in the semi-public forum provided by the MMC.

I believe the principal reason for this absence of Commission activity so far is the shift in bargaining power of the parties which I have described. The regulatory agenda has been that of winning back what is seen as excessive ground conceded at flotation, and the industries have mostly concluded that they do better to cede that ground than to submit to independent inquiry. But of course the more ground that is given, the less inclined utilities will be to give more. I predict that Sir Sydney will see many more references before long, and I suspect the first of them may not be far off.

How should the Commission react when these references occur? In all industries, the Commission has to strike a balance between the tightness of price control and the stimulation of competition. Should it protect consumers by pushing prices down, or will it do better to encourage entry by permitting relatively high prices to continue? That choice takes a different form in industries where entry is feasible or desirable - as it is in telecoms and electricity - from that which is appropriate where entry is unlikely. In both these industries, the likely costs of entry are far below the fully allocated costs of the incumbents, and the primary task of a competition authority is then to ensure that pricing policies do not reflect predatory intentions or predatory activities. The MMC's obligation in such cases is clear, although as the large literature on predation demonstrates, discharging that obligation is no easy task.

Sir Sydney has asked whether the RPI-X formula is the right system of price control. It is noticeable that this is one that is used by the Commission itself in other areas of regulation. While I share his concerns, I also go along with his conclusion that it is the least bad regulatory formula we have. I suspect we will move increasingly towards individual price caps, and that the way in which this regulatory model has evolved in telecoms is one which will be largely followed in other industries.

Let me offer another piece of unrequited advice. Sir Sydney asked in conclusion whether regulation would remain necessary indefinitely. I believe the ways in which effective competition across privatised utilities are likely to enable us to dispense with regulation to be worth discussing. It is clear that telecoms is in a real sense now like any other industry, in that a highly fragmented competitive structure is entirely feasible from a technical point of view. But what is feasible from a technical point of view is not necessarily what will occur. However, telecoms is by far the most potentially competitive of the utilities. In gas and electricity, parts - the supply business - may become almost wholly competitive if we try hard enough, but parts - transmission and distribution - are truly natural monopolies. And in water there is little prospect of any competition at all.

Nevertheless, the general direction of policy should be that of, as far as possible, making continuing regulation unnecessary. John Vickers and I have emphasised the distinction between structure and conduct regulation, the difference between protecting one's property by locking the door (a structural remedy) and asking the neighbours for assurances that they will not burgle the house (the conduct remedy). That comparison may bias the case but it fits my predisposition to favour structural remedies over conduct ones wherever possible.

I believe that is one of the lessons of Britain's privatisation experience. Almost without exception, restructuring and liberalisation have been resisted at the time of privatisation by the privatised utilities themselves. Yet it might be better for everyone, including the firms involved, if gas, and perhaps telecoms, had been suddenly butchered rather than subject to death by a thousand cuts. If instead they had been restructured at privatisation in ways that maximised the scope for competition, it is far more credible that the prospectuses which their managers believed they were offered - the opportunity to manage their businesses on commercial criteria applicable to any other firm - would have applied there as in any other industry.

4

USING COMPARATORS IN REGULATION

Mr. Alan Booker

Deputy Director General, OFWAT

Setting the Scene

IN COMPETITIVE MARKETS customers, managers and investors have a constant stream of information available to them to assist them in their respective rôles. Customers can respond to price and quality comparisons and trade off one aspect of choice against another. Managers can monitor their market share against their plans and respond by improving efficiency within the confines of their ability and the technology available, and again adjust quality and price in relation to market demands. Investors will respond to the profitability of the business in terms of their expectations and investment philosophy and again will respond accordingly. Each of these players will have different channels of communication which have developed in order to meet their needs in a sensitive and appropriate way.

In a regulated market the regulator, in his rôle as a surrogate for competition, needs to stimulate and promote these flows of information in a way which encourages customers, managers and investors to respond in a way which is not dissimilar from a competitive market. The regulator can then take these responses into account in his own rôle, such as during the review of price limits.

Regulated markets behave in different ways according to the degree of inherent competition. In water services, which are *de facto* total (local) monopolies at the present time, there is a need for significant information streams stimulated by the regulator. The other utilities are subject to a greater or lesser extent to some direct and increasing competition following some prodding from their regulators and may need less information stimulus from their regulators. The structure of the industry also has a substantial bearing on the requirement for comparators. For instance, water supply is operated by 32 separate regional companies widely ranged in size, whilst there are just 10 large sewerage companies each of which is comparable in size to the regional electricity companies but small by comparison with British Gas or BT. Because of the number of companies operating in the water services industry it is possible to develop comparative competition; I will be saying something of how far we have progressed.

I want to concentrate on the water services area because that is the industry I know best. But I do have some information from other regulated industries to draw on. The limitation, however, is in the use of published data as opposed to being able to draw on all the information provided to the regulator in confidence. The approach which I want to take is to follow the lines of a communication analysis following the what, why, where, when and who format and by showing examples at appropriate stages.

What Comparators?

Charges

Probably the first point of comparison which customers make concerns charges, particularly in an industry like water where there are a number of regional companies to compare. Although within the present arrangements customers have very limited opportunity to choose where they take their water supply from or where they dispose of their sewage, they are nevertheless very interested in the different charges which are made in different areas. Table 1 shows this comparison and indicates a wide spread of charges for essentially the same service. So although such a league table is helpful it does not tell the whole story and in the past companies have been able to hide behind a range of 'explanatory factors'.

TABLE 1:
AVERAGE HOUSEHOLD BILLS FOR UNMEASURED SEWERAGE, 1992/93

COMPANY	% Increase 1989/90 - 1990/91	%Increase 1990/91 - 1991/92	%Increase 1991/92 - 1992/93	Levels From April 1992 £
Anglian Water Services Ltd.	7.3	12.5	9.3	121
Dwr Cymru Cyfyngedig				
(Welsh Water)	9.7	16.3	8.7	99
North West Water Ltd.	12.5	14.5	9.7	83
Northumbrian Water Ltd.	19.5	16.5	10.7	85
Severn Trent Water Ltd.	12.9	14.8	9.4	84
South West Water Services Ltd.	12.2	17.1	23.1	135
Southern Water Services Ltd.	10.3	15.0	9.4	102
Thames Water Utilities Ltd.	10.3	14.4	11.5	69
Wessex Water Services Ltd.	11.2	13.0	8.4	105
Yorkshire Water Services Ltd.	9.8	12.6	9.5	81

In the water industry there is general agreement even by the regulator that there are some valid reasons for there to be a diversity of charges for essentially the same service because of diverse costs. Some of these reasons are natural factors such as geography, topography and concentration of population. There are other factors such as the age of the assets, ranging from old early Victorian cities to new towns with assets doing the same job but at different initial costs and different efficiencies. This leads naturally to the need to use total costs for comparative purposes and for a common currency of comparison through the use of current cost accounting.

Service

Under the terms of water and sewerage licences the Director General has a duty to collect and publish information about standards of service. Table 2 shows the current list of levels of service indicators.

The information company by company is published annually in a Levels of Service report and broken down by region. Table 3 shows the response to billing queries for the Thames region.

TABLE 2:
LEVELS OF SERVICE INDICATORS

DG1	**Raw Water Availability** identifies the population whose calculated water resource availability is below the reference level.
DG2	**Pressure of Mains Water** identifies the number of customers' properties that are at risk of receiving mains water pressure that is below the reference level.
DG3	**Interruptions to Water Supplies** identifies the number of customers' properties that have experienced a loss of supply for longer than the reference level, without reasonable notice from the company.
DG4	**Water Usage Restrictions** identifies the population who have been subject to water usage restrictions.
DG5	**Flooding from Sewers** identifies the number of customers' properties where the risk of flooding from public sewers is worse than the reference level.
DG6	**Response to Billing Queries** identifies the banded response time for meaningful responses to customers' billing queries.
DG7	**Response to Written Complaints** identifies the banded response time for meaningful responses to customers' written complaints.

The problem with levels of service information for a large number of regulated companies is that the information becomes voluminous and quite complicated. I think we need to consider alternative methods of presentation. For instance, regional leaflets may be a more useful alternative to national reports.

A further difficulty is the consistency of the information. The annual reports from companies are independently certified by technical and financial auditors who ascribe confidence grades to the information provided by companies. Confidence grades are based on both reliability and accuracy but with such a wide variation in confidence levels that the information has to be used with caution. Over time it is expected that all companies will achieve high confidence grades but until that time the variation in confidence grades is a comparator which the regulator will take into account.

TABLE 3:
RESPONSE TO BILLING QUERIES:
ASSESSMENT OF PERFORMANCE 1990/91

Thames Region

Region Company	Percentage Responses in each band					Assessment of Company Performance 1991/91
	Band 1	Band 2	Band 3	Band 4	Band 5	
East Surrey	96	1	1	<1	2	Good
Mid Southern	67	8	12	12	<1	Moderate
North Surrey	78	13	7	1	<1	Very Good
Sutton District	78	8	6	6	<3	Good
Thames	48	16	19	12	3	Poor
Three Valleys:						
Colne Valley	40	24	16	14	6	Poor
Lee Valley	53	15	14	12	6	Poor
Rickmansworth	87	6	4	2	1	Good

Band 1 less than 2 working days
Band 2 more than 2 but less than 5 working days
Band 3 more than 5 but less than 10 working days
Band 4 more than 10 but less than 20 working days
Band 5 more than 20 working days.

Why Have Comparators?

As I have indicated, the principal reason for making comparisons is to help in the simulation of the market. Money markets make continuous assessment of companies' performance and prospects assisted by reports from analysts. These reports in themselves are extremely valuable sources of information for regulators both forming and reporting market perceptions of company performance. So the assessment of performance is important from the point of view of all three constituents which regulators have to be responsive towards: customers, managers and investors.

The Director General of Water Services has a primary responsibility to ensure that an efficient company can properly finance its functions so he has an imperative to assess efficiency. This can only be done on the basis of performance in terms of cost and service. Efficiency measurement demands a comparison between inputs and outputs. From a customer's point of view the inputs are the income stream which he is providing in return for the products and services he receives. The linkage between inputs and outputs will always be an imperfect one but it is important for regulators to develop an understanding of those linkages.

In water we have chosen water delivered to customers as the principal water service output of the companies. It is perhaps a little surprising that the industry has never in the past habitually measured the amount of water it supplies to its customers. In the past the concentration has been on the amount of water supplied into the network rather than the amount which comes out at the other end of the network. Perhaps this is not surprising in view of the amount of water which is lost in between the treatment works and the customer. Figures of up to 40 per cent are not uncommon in some parts of companies' networks and overall in England and Wales the figure is of the order of 25 per cent.

TABLE 4:
WATER DELIVERED: COMPARATIVE DATA, 1990/91

South East Region

COMPANY	COMPARATIVE DATA			
	Water Delivered (% WS)	U/m household per capita (l/h/d)	U/m non-household (l/prop/d) (% WD)	
S1	80	159	1514	3
S2	82	175	746	1
S3	76	150	2667	4
S4	83	251	1250	3
S5	76	169	843	1
S6	76	175	2200	8
S7	73	153	932	2
S8	77	183	0	0
S9	83	167	7077	2
S10	77	156	540	1
S11	78	158	1000	1
S12	75	174	600	2
S13	71	154	395	2

WS   Waste Supplied
U/m   Unmeasured consumption
l/h/d   Litres per household per day
l/prop/d   Litres per property per day
WD   Water Delivered

The difficulty in measuring water delivered to customers is that only about one-third of all water delivered is measured. This is principally to business and commercial customers. The metering of domestic customers has only recently become an issue following the 1989 Water Act where the legislation allowed water companies to use the old rateable values for charging purposes until the year 2000 when some alternative basis needs to be found. Following the OFWAT consultation on Paying for Water the most likely way forward is an extension of domestic water metering on a selective basis. This process needs to reflect the economics of developing new water resources compared with meter installation to help reduce leakage and to manage average and peak demand downwards. Until such time as all water delivered is measured, estimates of usage by certain groups of unmeasured customers needs to be part of the methodology for water delivered. Table 4 shows the data for all the water companies in the South East region on an anonymised basis.

TABLE 5:
WATER DELIVERED: Unit Costs, 1990/91

South East Region

UNIT COSTS						
Company	Optg cost	CC Dep Inf Ren Charge (p/cub.m)	Current Cost Op Prof (p/cub.m)	Full Capital Charge (p/cub.m)	Total Cost 1	Total Cost 2
	(p/cub.m)				(p/cub.m)	(p/cub.m)
S1	20	7	5	54	33	82
S2	24	6	9	47	39	78
S3	25	12	4	54	41	91
S4	25	14	7	79	48	120
S5	27	11	5	49	42	86
S6	29	5	19	55	53	88
S7	29	11	21	79	60	118
S8	32	4	10	42	46	78
S9	32	10	4	97	46	139
S10	42	11	5	85	58	138
S11	43	30	10	154	80	224
S12	44	22	12	93	78	158
S13	51	21	4	97	77	170

Optg - Operating
CC Dept Inf Ren - Current Cost Depreciation, continuous renewal
p/cub.m - pence per cubic metre

Moving on, Table 5 shows the costs of the companies in Table 4 related to the water delivered. Costs are calculated as total current costs and an examination of these shows a significant variation between companies. In the past companies have explained away these differences by 'explanatory factors'.

Such factors make an interesting area for comparison between companies and may have significant implications for costs and outputs in water and sewerage services. Table 6 lists the principal explanatory factors which have so far been identified as having some influence on

TABLE 6:
EXPLANATORY FACTORS

				Actuals			
				Reporting Year 1991/92			
Row Nr	BoN Ref	(1)	Item Description	Units Nr	C G	%	C G
01		I	Sources - Impounding reservoirs				
02		I	Sources - River abstractions				
03		I	Sources - Boreholes				
04		I	Sources - Bulk supplies (raw)				
05		I	Sources - Bulk supplies (treated)				
06		I	Works size <0.99 Ml/d				
07		I	Works size 1-4.99 Ml/d				
08		I	Works size 5-24.00 Ml/d				
09		I	Works size 25-99.99 Ml/d				
10		I	Works size >100 Ml/d				
11		I	Tment. type - Surface physical				
12		I	Tment. type - Surface phys. + chem.				
13		I	Tment. type - Surface additional				
14		I	Tment. type - Ground simple				
15		I	Tment. type - Ground complex single				
16		I	Tment. type - Ground complex multi				
17		I	Peak volume (index)				
18		I	Average pumping head (metres)				

Note (1) 'I' refers to input row
Undertaker: Signed:
Responsible Officers: Date:

water costs. There is a similar set of factors for sewage. Although such factors as the pumping level would quite readily be accepted as influencing operating costs, it is not easy to develop algorithms which can be modelled. We do, however, hope that as the quality of information on cost ratios gets better and as we develop our thinking on explanatory factors, it will be feasible to devise a tenable modelling methodology.

In the short term it is our intention to publish, in an attributed way, unit costs of water delivered later this year after analysis of the annual returns from companies in July.

Comparative Competition

The theme of comparative (or yardstick) competition is one which has run since the earliest days of privatisation of the water industry. It is an idea which is complementary to direct competition rather than a replacement for it and whilst the longer-term scope for competition in water will be determined by our ability to develop a suitable approach to common carriage, there will inevitably be a need to retain regulation of the network.

Comparative competition is a concept which means a variety of things. From a regulatory point of view it means creating a wholly transparent flow of information to customers, money markets, managers and the regulator about company performance and efficiency. This information is then used periodically by the regulator in setting efficiency targets for incorporation in price limits, by customers in making judgements about the standard of service they receive, by investors in determining investment risk, and by managers in improving management practices and company policies. It is a process or concept which reaches into every nook and cranny of the business sector and the individual company. The effectiveness of the process rests on the publication of information and the ability of the different parties to respond to that information.

One of the problems in the early years of the privatised water industry is to distinguish between what has been done in terms of work and investment and what has been achieved in terms of improved quality of service, product and environment. In many ways commentators have been happy to see water companies increasing their investment and to equate increased investment in a vague way with increased standards of service.

Table 7 demonstrates the comparison between the planned and actual investment programme of the industry. On the other hand, customers who are funding this investment through price increases running at around 5 per cent a year in real terms are understandably looking for improvements in water quality, service levels and environmental improvements, all of which are slow to show through in the information which we have available.

TABLE 7:
EXPENDITURE AND VARIANCE FOR EACH SERVICE CATEGORY, 1990/91, AND FORECAST + ACTUAL EXPENDITURE, 1989/90 TO 1994/95

1990/92 prices	1990/91		1989/90 to 1994/95	
	Actual expenditure £M	Variance from licence BoN £M	Forecast + actual expenditure £M	Variance from licence BoN £M
Water resources	113	4	722	55
Water treatment	287	-39	2,571	288
Water distribution	619	2	3,869	-14
Management and general (water)	173	22	1,103	246
Sewage	429	-28	2,930	-31
Sewerage treatment	732	-9	5,041	753
Management and general (sewerage)	151	11	981	168
TOTAL	2,504	-36	17,216	1,464

BoN - Book of Numbers

Table 8 lists the price limit (K) factors which apply to the water companies up to the year 2000. These K factors are at present only subject to the licence conditions and to companies carrying out agreed investment programmes rather than to the explicit achievement of service improvements. At the Periodic Review of price limits in 1994 it is the intention of the Director General to make the régime more output orientated and to seek active customer involvement in the process. This will allow customers to express views about price increases, and about possible trade-offs with service improvements. These will be set in the context of specific proposals from companies in discretionary areas and it will be interesting to see how company priorities can be affected by factors such as affordability and willingness to pay.

TABLE 8:
K FACTORS: BY WATER COMPANY, 1992/93 TO 1999/2000

	92/93	93/94	94/95	95/96	96/97	97/98	98/99	99/00
Anglian	5.5	5.5	5.5	5.5	5.5	5.5	5.5	5.5
Bournemouth	15.0	0.0	0.0	0.0	0.0	0.0	0.0	0.0
Bristol	4.0	4.0	2.0	2.0	2.0	2.0	2.0	2.0
Cambridge	8.0	0.0	0.0	0.0	-2.0	-2.0	-2.0	-2.0
Chester	4.5	1.0	1.0	1.0	1.0	1.0	1.0	1.0
Cholderton	6.0	6.0	6.0	6.0	6.0	6.0	6.0	6.0
Dwr Cymru	6.5	6.5	6.5	5.5	5.5	5.5	5.5	5.5.
East Worcs	11.0	11.0	-1.0	-1.0	-1.0	-1.0	-1.0	-1.0
East Surrey	2.0	2.0	2.0	2.0	2.0	2.0	2.0	2.0
East Anglian	13.0	13.0	3.0	1.0	1.0	1.0	1.0	1.0
Essex	5.0	5.0	5.0	4.5	4.5	4.5	4.5	4.5
Folkestone	8.0	8.0	8.0	8.0	0.0	0.0	0.0	0.0
Hartlepools	3.5	3.5	3.5	3.5	3.5	3.5	3.5	3.5
Mid Kent	2.5	2.5	2.5	2.5	2.5	2.5	2.5	2.5
Mid Southern	10.0	4.0	4.0	4.0	0.0	0.0	0.0	0.0
North East Water	6.0	3.0	3.0	2.0	2.0	2.0	2.0	2.0
North Surrey	8.5	8.5	8.5	2.0	2.0	2.0	2.0	2.0
North West	5.0	5.0	5.0	5.0	5.0	5.0	5.0	5.0
Northumbrian	7.0	7.0	7.0	3.0	3.0	3.0	3.0	3.0
Portsmouth	5.5	5.5	2.0	2.0	2.0	2.0	2.0	2.0
Severn Trent	5.5	5.5	5.5	2.0	2.0	2.0	2.0	2.0
South East Water	8.0	2.5	0.0	0.0	0.0	0.0	0.0	0.0
South Staffs	5.0	3.0	3.0	2.0	2.0	2.0	2.0	2.0
South West	6.5	6.5	6.5	5.5	5.5	5.5	5.5	5.5
Southern	5.5	3.5	3.5	0.0	0.0	0.0	0.0	0.0
Sutton	8.5	8.5	3.5	3.5	3.5	3.5	3.5	3.5
Tendring Hundred	13.0	13.0	2.5	2.5	2.5	2.5	2.5	2.5
Thames	4.5	4.5	4.5	4.5	4.5	4.5	4.5	4.5
Thames Valleys	4.0	1.6	1.5	1.5	1.5	1.5	0.2	0.2
Wessex	4.5	4.5	4.5	4.5	4.5	4.5	4.5	4.5
West Hampshire	7.5	7.5	5.5	5.5	5.5	5.5	5.5	5.5
Wrexham	15.0	0.0	0.0	0.0	0.0	0.0	0.0	0.0
York	3.0	3.0	3.0	3.0	3.0	3.0	3.0	3.0
Yorkshire	3.0	3.0	3.0	3.0	3.0	3.0	3.0	3.0

When to Have Comparators?

The simple answer here is that there needs to be a regular flow of information to allow the regulator and the various interested parties to form views. Much of the information can only be collected and analysed on an annual basis. This includes the financial performance of companies taken from the annual regulatory accounts, and information such as disconnection statistics and levels of service indicators taken from annual returns.

Some information is only worth publishing periodically and Table 9 shows an example of this kind of comparison which will probably concentrate on service levels, and show up improvements or deterioration over time. Such comparisons may be undertaken every three or four years to provide a periodic snapshot of a particular situation. It is quite usual, however, for quality of service information to be produced as a time series to show trends. Table 10 shows an example of this type of information. Such a detailed report showing the comparison over time of one company's performance is helpful both from a regulatory, management and customer viewpoint, but in the water sector such reports produced annually for each of 32 companies would provide so much detailed data that the significance would largely be lost. The nature of the business and the structure of the industry are likely to determine the scope of service comparisons.

TABLE 9:
TIME TAKEN BETWEEN FIRST CONTACT AND SERVICE/REPAIR VISIT:
BRITISH GAS, 1981 AND 1989

	BRITISH GAS	
	1981 %	1989 %
Same day	13	20
1 to 2 days	19	19
3 to 4 days	16	12
5 to 10 days	27	21
11 to 14 days	4	3
15 to 30 days	4	3
1 month later or more	4	4
Don't know/not stated	13	17
Base	1,140	706

Source: Consumer Policy Review, June 1992.

TABLE 10:
BT'S QUALITY OF SERVICE RESULTS, 1985-1987

MEASUREMENT PERCENTAGE OF:-	RESULT	
	1985-86	Sept. 1987
Faults (serious) cleared within 2 working days	87.10[1]	86.50
Business order completed within 6 working days	60.80	43.30
Residential orders completed within 8 working days	59.40	42.50
Operator calls answered within 15 seconds	85.60	79.40
Directory enquiry calls answered within 15 seconds	74.00	75.10
Local calls failed because of network faults or congestion	1.70	2.20
Trunk calls failed because of network faults or congestion	4.10	4.30
Faults, per line per year, network and customer equipment	0.48%	0.43%
Faults, per line per year, network only	0.20%	0.20%

[1] End of next working day.
Source: BT, *Quality of service report*, 1987.

Where Should Comparators be Published?

Within the Company

Before privatisation BT published quality of service information in its annual report; however, after privatisation it discontinued the publication of these indicators on the grounds of commercial confidentiality. The regulator was not impressed and in November 1986 published his first report on the quality of telephone service. BT resumed publication of its own measures in October 1987. There was strong public perception that BT's level of service quality was inadequate and the company was forced into a position where for the pay phone service at least it had to produce target levels of service and a viable plan to meet them. BT now produces a quality of service report every six months and although there is an explicit target for pay phone availability the company's figures do not in general specify what level of service performance the company is trying to achieve in aggregate.

Major Issues in Regulation

This example is an interesting one where the public and the regulator, working together, forced the monopoly company to adopt a course of action which it had decided against. The Competition and Service (Utilities) Act 1992 now gives quite powerful messages to the utility companies. For instance, all four utility regulators are given powers to ensure that the companies inform customers about the standards set for them and how well the company has performed over all standards. This power will, I am sure, lead to all utility companies, operating in all four sectors, water, gas, telecommunications and electricity, providing information about targets and achievements each year to customers.

Within the Industry

Where there is comparative information available to regulators across a specific regulated sector there are already mechanisms for information to be published either by the regulator or by a body such as the Centre for the Study of Regulated Industries (CRI). An example of this kind of information is the annual CRI publication covering charges for water services. This document is produced primarily as a reference document rather than as a customer-friendly publication and gives a detailed analysis of water charges and tariff structures company by company. The degree of detail is exemplified in Table 11, which tabulates specimen measured sewerage bills for different quantities of water used and serves to demonstrate the variability between companies both in terms of the standing charges which vary by a factor of 2 and volumetric charges by a factor of 3.

Other Comparisons

So far I have talked about the use of comparators within the company and within the regulated industry. Such comparisons are invaluable in creating a régime of incentive regulation. However, they do have their limitations. They are essentially comparisons of groupings isolated from the general economy within a country. League tables based on performance comparison between utility companies in the same sector can at best only show relativities between companies in that sector, and in order to demonstrate absolute levels of performance it is necessary to look outside the specific regulated sector under scrutiny.

It is useful therefore to consider comparisons running across regulated sectors. Such comparisons would of course need to be in comparable

TABLE 11:
MEASURED SEWERAGE CHARGES

Measured sewerage: charges: specimen household bills	Tariffs 1991/92 Complete Sewerage			Consumption per year		
	Domestic standing charge £	RV Charge per/£ RV	Water in= water out volume charge p/cu.m	1 person household 65 cu.m £	2 person household 115 cu.m £	4 person household 185 cu.m £
Anglian	38.0		60.46	79.96	107.19	149.51
Dwr Cymru Cyfyngedig	49.0		66.51	92.23	125.49	172.04
North West*	56.00		32.90	77.39	93.84	116.87
Northumbrian*	0.00	17.74	27.18	53.15	66.74	85.76
Severn Trent*						
Zone 1	0.00	18.43	32.54	58.01	74.28	97.06
Zone 2	0.00	15.53	32.54	52.21	68.48	91.26
Zone 3	0.00	16.45	32.54	54.05	70.32	93.10
Zone 4	0.00	17.76	32.54	56.67	72.94	95.72
Zone 5	0.00	20.78	32.54	62.71	78.98	101.76
Zone 6	0.00	20.12	32.54	61.39	77.66	100.44
Zone 7	0.00	19.60	32.54	60.35	76.62	99.40
Zone 8	0.00	16.45	32.54	54.05	70.32	93.10
South West	44.00		85.22	99.39	142.00	201.66
Southern	35.00		56.15	71.50	99.57	138.88
Thames	25.00		33.01	46.46	62.96	86.07
Wessex	36.50		60.94	76.11	106.58	149.24
Yorkshire	32.00		70.87	78.07	113.50	163.11

*for areas where a Rateable Value (RV) charge is made rather than a fixed standing charge, an RV of £200 has been assumed.
p/cu.m = pence per cubic metre.

areas of activity, and many service measures can sensibly be compared across utility industries. For instance, response to complaints about billing could form a useful guide to the performance of the different utility sectors. Similarly, there are a range of activities in regulated industries which are carried out in other industries, such as laying pipes and ducts, or operating a fleet of vehicles. Consistency is always going to be a problem for these types of comparisons but nevertheless it does not mean that they should be automatically ruled out. Such comparisons are not done at present but they could form a useful area of study for interested academics.

It is also beneficial to carry out international comparisons. National Utility Services Limited (NUS) provides energy, water and telecommunications cost analyses to three-quarters of a million businesses world-wide. Table 12 shows their international league tables for water in 1990 and 1991, and gives the relative positions of the 13 highest priced countries and the percentage increase by comparison with the rate of inflation. For instance, the UK moved up from 9th position in 1990 to 6th position in 1991 with a real rate of increase of almost $9^1/2$ per cent. Again, consistency of data is always going to be a problem, and although there are some technical problems with the NUS figures, such comparisons do have a part to play in the perceptions of customers and therefore of regulators.

TABLE 12:
INTERNATIONAL WATER PRICE SURVEY

LEAGUE TABLE						
1990			1991			
PLACE	COUNTRY	P/M3	COUNTRY	P/M3	INC%	RPI%
1	Australia	84.17	Australia	87.72	4.21	4.8
2	Germany*	70.24	Germany*	72.39	3.06	3.0
3	Italy	58.89	Italy	70.42	19.57	6.6
4	France	52.23	France	54.94	5.19	3.2
5	Belgium	50.02	Finland	52.78	5.88	4.8
6	Finland	49.85	UK	48.14	15.22	5.8
7	Netherlands	45.22	Netherlands	45.92	1.55	3.3
8	Sweden	42.05	Belgium	44.00	(12.02)	3.2
9	UK	41.78	Sweden	43.51	3.47	10.4
10	Eire	28.76	Eire	29.26	1.74	3.1
11	US	23.84	US	27.51	15.37	5.0
12	Canada	20.18	Canada	22.07	9.39	6.2
13	Norway	17.41	Norway	17.41	0.00	3.8

Figures in brackets indicate price decrease.
*Figures are for the western part of Germany only.
P/M3 - pence per cubic metre.
RPI% - Percentage increase in Retail Price Index.

TABLE 13:
COMPLAINT STATISTICS BY COMPANY FOR THE PERIOD 1 APRIL 1990 TO
31 MARCH 1991

Company	Number of Complaints Received	Complaints per 100,000 Customers
East Worcestershire	61	66.3
East Surrey	64	50.4
Mid Sussex	49	48.0
Cambridge	43	38.2
West Kent	20	35.1
South Staffordshire	153	32.3
Welsh Water	362	30.0
Eastbourne	30	29.6
Suffolk	32	29.3
Mid Kent	59	27.3
Yorkshire	516	25.9
Severn Trent	855	25.6
South West	165	25.0
North East	132	23.4
York	16	21.9
Tending Hundred	14	21.6
North West	614	21.0
Bristol	82	19.0
Wrexham	11	18.3
Wessex	162	17.4
West Hampshire	10	13.3
Mid Southern	35	12.9
Northumbrian	139	12.6
Anglian	277	12.5
Southern	190	11.3
Three Valleys	101	10.6
Portsmouth	28	10.4
Bournemouth	8	8.2
Sutton	9	7.7
Essex	45	7.6
Thames	355	6.6
Folkestone	4	6.0
Hartlepools	2	5.4
Chester	2	4.7
North Surrey	8	4.5
Cholderton	0	0
National Average	4,633	17.5

Who Should Make Comparisons?

Customers

There is a legitimate rôle for customer organisations to carry out comparisons. In the case of business and industrial customers there are well-established organisations such as the Energy Information Centre which produce regular comparisons of prices across companies. Customer service organisations such as the water CSCs also have a remit in this area. Comparisons of disconnections and levels of complaint are typical of the interest of CSCs. Table 13 shows a comparison of complaints figures across the different CSC areas and shows a wide variation in complaints levels. Similarly, the disconnection statistics shown in Table 14 are also indicative of levels of service. In the case of water it is not easy to discern what such figures are indicating, with a wide variety of disconnection policies operative between companies. At one extreme of the spectrum, companies will not disconnect domestic customers under any circumstances, whilst at the other extreme companies have a strict disconnection policy following systematic procedures on the collection of debt. However, it is clear that the overall level of debt in water companies is increasing substantially as bills increase in real terms year after year. Superimpose this picture on increasing levels of unemployment and a complex picture emerges. Comparisons are quite often invidious.

TABLE 14:
NUMBER OF DOMESTIC DISCONNECTIONS BY REGION FOR EACH SIX
MONTHS FROM 1/4/89 - 30/9/91

	1/4/91- 30/9/91	1/10/91- 31/3/91	1/4/90- 30/3/90	1/10/89- 31/3/90	1/4/89- 30/9/89
Central	1,199	249	213	323	1,024
Anglian	972	774	197	65	1,191
North West	1,223	508	381	344	412
Northumbrian	362	501	161	192	529
South West	241	91	119	73	172
Southern	383	90	339	206	713
Thames	663	579	387	174	513
Wales	1,410	665	640	692	664
Wessex	219	150	44	10	130
Yorkshire	990	941	644	445	554
TOTALS	7,662	4,548	3,125	2,524	5,902

Investors

Investment analysts regularly produce detailed assessments of company performance to assist investors. Such information as that shown in Table 15 is valuable also from a regulatory point of view in the assessment of appropriate rates of return. The cost of capital will be of on-going interest to regulators as competition for investment continues to be the principal element of direct competition in some regulated industries such as water. These kinds of comparisons are also useful background information during price reviews, since the regulator has to have regard to a range of financial indicators under the terms of the licence. Such information produced by the City or by the media is different from that produced by the regulator in terms of price sensitivity. Regulators need to be constantly aware of the City's reaction to information they publish and to handle it appropriately.

TABLE 15:
(a) CITY COMPARATORS

	pence per share 15.4.92	pence per share 1992		Mkt. Cap £m.	Yld Gross Div	
	Price	High	Low			P/E
Anglian	416	423	308¹/₂	1,227	5.6	8.6
Bristol	605	605	485	35.7	1.5	15.5
East Surrey	225	225	200	28.3	4.7	6.3
Mid Kent	173	173	163	29.4	6.9	4.9
North West	418	425	323	1,488	5.7	7.4
Northumbrian	432	440	336	287.6	5.7	5.5
Severn Trent	382	390	298	1,352	6.1	5.9
Southern	384	394	301	631.6	6.1	6.4
South Staffs	750	750	670	40.3	1.9	7.3
South West	403	406	306	499.1	6.6	6.1
Thames	426	430	324	1,648	5.5	8.7
Welsh	434	443	337	627.6	6.0	5.2
Wessex	463	465	366	476.7	5.1	7.3
Yorkshire	437	445	336	862.7	5.4	7.9

TABLE 15:
(b) UTILITY COMPARATORS

Wednesday 15 April 1992						Year ago (approx)
Equity Groups & Sub-Sections	Index No.	Est Earnings Yield % (Max)	Gross Div Yield % (Act at 25%)	Est P/E Ratio (Net)	xd adj 1992 to date	Index No
Electricity (16)	1,267.63	13.86	5.63	9.41	17.21	1,186.40
Telephone Networks (4)	1,429.52	10.97	4.39	11.91	16.02	1,466.31
Water (10)	2,740.18	15.56	5.80	7.08	0.00	2,532.58
Oil & Gas (17)	2,088.68	7.47	6.81	17.66	41.53	2,430.35

Figures in parentheses show number of stocks per section.

Management

There is clearly an on-going educational and information rôle for management to provide usable information to customers. One area of comparison for regulators is the willingness of companies to publish meaningful information for customers about services available and about how costs are moving and why. In a business such as water, subject to an RPI + K price limit, where K is running at around 5, it is incumbent upon companies to explain clearly to customers why that is so and what they are getting for increased prices. For most customers there will be little to see and no guarantee of value for money. Many customers genuinely cannot follow the arguments. They see prices increase, they hear of poor water quality, and of pollution in the rivers and on the beaches, they hear of increased water company profits and higher chairmen's salaries. Some then go on to demand to know what the regulators are going to do about it. So there is a major education and information need which companies have not yet properly addressed. There is a limit to how persuasive you can be in telling people how much water they can get for the price of a bar of chocolate. Such comparisons can be helpful but they do not give an absolute sense of what increases in quality and environmental standards are being bought through the water bill. Companies need to develop their thinking significantly in this area.

The Regulators

So what is left for the regulator to do? I have outlined some of the areas

82

of legitimate interest for regulators to compare performance and to publish information. Those areas of interest are many and regulators need to use great skill in the selection of appropriate information for publication, by comparison with the information which is retained on a confidential basis for assessing performance. For instance in water information is currently being sought on activity costs. Such volumes of information across 32 companies would be difficult to publish in a helpful format. But of course, it will underlie more high level performance comparisons such as unit cost comparisons. Inconsistencies between performance indicated by unit costs and activity costings will need to be explored; ultimately I am confident that the collection of such detailed information will give a better understanding of the cost structure of different companies and the relationship to explanatory factors. However, there is a balance which regulators need to strike in demands for information from regulated industries. The powers available are substantial but there is a price tag to this kind of information as with every other type of demand, and a balance needs to be struck between the cost of producing information purely for the regulator and its place in the rôle of the regulator. This place is likely to be rather personal to individual regulators and their style of regulation.

Summary

I have summarised the matrix of use of comparators in Table 16 as a cross-check against the different elements as I see them. I have already

TABLE 16:
SUMMARY MATRIX OF COMPARATORS

WHY	WHAT	WHO	WHEN	WHERE
Comparative competition	Prices	Regulator	Regular flow	Published
Efficiency targets	Costs	Customers	Annual	CRI, CSC
Incentive regulation	Outputs	Investors	Time series	User associations
Market simulation	Performance	Managers		Annual reports
Price limits	Service	Academics		Pamphlets
	Other industries			Regional
	International			Press releases
	Financial			Price sensitive

indicated my conviction that the use of comparators is a personal matter based in the style of the regulator and I firmly believe this to be so. However, I find it difficult to accept that a regulator could do an adequate job without a minimum level of comparison across the regulated business. Where regulation is confined to the common carriage network it is feasible to limit the areas of comparison to that regulated element, and as more direct competition opens up in regulated utilities over the coming years it may be possible to draw even better comparisons between the different networks.

I believe the use of comparators in regulation is still in its infancy. Whilst the linkages between costs and outputs are imperfectly understood the use of comparators will be an inexact science, but I am firmly convinced that as regulation becomes more sophisticated the use of sophisticated comparisons will become second nature. I am looking forward to helping to make it so.

USING COMPARISONS IN REGULATION

DISCUSSANT:
Mr. A. J. Meyrick*

H.M. Treasury

FOLLOWING LIEBENSTEIN, it was always known that some form of efficiency contract was necessary to bolster the regulation of monopolies which would otherwise have little incentive to surrender organisational comfort in favour of rooting out inefficiency and investing in technical progress. At the same time it was also known that an efficiency audit based on a single source of information would be heavily flawed: on the one hand, it would risk simply endorsing the organisation's own costs in a simple price pass through; on the other, it risked confiscating the profit reward that should follow cost-reducing managerial innovation.

In the UK, OFWAT have taken the lead in developing yardstick comparators in which data supplied by the various water undertakings on their costs and efficiency can be used as a general efficiency audit to help the Regulator to reset price caps without the incentive penalties which would follow from using a single organisation's own performance data. Many thanks are therefore due to Alan Booker for the insights into OFWAT's thinking about the use of comparators and the data now being assembled.

*A.J. Meyrick is Senior Economic Adviser in the Government Economic Service. The views expressed here are the author's own.

85

General approaches to regulation of utilities have identified four styles of regulation:

o   Encouraging rapid emergence of competitive contestability;

o   Rate of return control;

o   Price cap regulation;

o   Management franchise by periodic competitive tender.

None of these styles is readily applicable to the water service industry in the UK. *Contestability* is not generally practicable, though there may be some possibilities in borderline locations and more may develop in time, especially for large water users. *Rate of return control* would be almost impossible to pursue in an arm's length way, because of the discrepancy between the market value of assets and their much greater replacement costs on a modern equivalent asset basis. *Price cap regulation* is only readily applicable for an industry which has previously been running on a broadly even keel, so that the counterfactual can be reasonably projected. In the case of water, the previous failure fully to maintain and replace capital and the shift in water quality regulations meant this counterfactual was difficult to project, and the K factors were broadly established on the basis of non-competitive negotiation with incumbent management. *Periodic competitive tender for management control* was ruled out prior to privatisation. Subsequent take-over auctions, in which lower K values have been negotiated, have provided some of this.

In the unusual circumstances of the water industry, the regulatory framework has been a mixture of these strategies. And data supplied by the water undertakings on the quality and quantity of the services they provided, their costs and efficiency are growing influences on the Regulator's price decisions.

The problem with getting simple yardstick comparators, for example, like those in Mr Booker's Table 1, Table 5 and Table 12, is that each company then insists that its costs differ because its background circumstances of natural geography, population density and state of assets differ.

Comparators required by the economic regulator need to be carefully selected to provide just enough information for him to be able to judge the extent to which the companies are delivering their side of the bargain. Comparators inevitably provide incentives for the companies to skew their managerial attention to improving their performance in the activities measured.

In this respect, the list of levels of service indicators in Table 2 looks to be oddly focussed on quantity indicators rather than quality of water delivered and effects on the environment. The former is what consumers are most interested in, and the two together underlie the need for the substantial capital programme which was the reason for the large real increases in water charges and taxes.

Water services are highly capital intensive, as indicated in Tables 5 and 7. In this context, it seems desirable to have some intermediate output measures of the companies' achievements in improving their capital stock. Simply measuring the level of capital expenditure is inadequate. Nor, because of lags, can you expect to pick up the results in final output measures of water quality.

In focussing on attempts to achieve valid comparisons, it is important not to lose sight of time-series data, for example, relating to:

o   overall manning and productivity;

o   unit costs of particular standard functions such as billing, maintenance;

o   success in reducing management overheads;

o   rate of return on capital employed.

There are obvious reasons why the levels of such measures are likely to vary between companies because of their different physical endowments and geography. Nevertheless, it might be useful to OFWAT to compare trends as an indicator of managerial success.

Mr Booker refers to the difficulties of assembling large numbers of performance indicators and presenting them in an intelligible way to allow realistic impressions of service to be drawn. In this area it may well be worth investigating the possibilities for using modern techniques of statistical analysis and cost-benefit analysis to provide weighted averages of performance. Some limited use of modelling could contribute to the explanation of significant areas of cross-company variance in costs of particular activities.

The developing system of OFWAT is yet a long way from providing simple yardsticks which would allow price caps to be reset on the basis of generalised information about achievable efficiency gains without subsequently penalising high achievers. However, it may be possible to generate some standard benchmarks on the basis of accounting costs 'to correct' for the geographical cost differences faced by individual water undertakings to overcome the objections outlined in paragraph 6 above.

I am pleased to see from Mr Booker's paper that information is now being sought from the companies on activity costs (see above, page 83). Many such activities can be identified which have a large measure of commonality with other companies and other public utilities and can therefore provide good partial indicators of performance, for example, billing costs, costs of laying pipes and digging trenches, running vehicle fleets, etc. Mr Booker is, however, right to warn us of the costs of data requirements in terms of management and compliance costs. It is also important that the economic regulation of the industry does not weaken the powers and responsibilities of managers to manage.

Issues for Discussion

It seems to me that there are four main areas for discussion:

o   To what extent can capital market competition and competition for control, for example by mergers, substitute for regulation and efficiency audit in spurring efficiency?

o   Can modelling help to convert the high-level indicators of unit costs into realistic, but simple, yardsticks for comparing overall efficiency?

o   Can the array of comparators be more tightly focussed on those which are relevant to ascertaining the efficiency of management and the scope for improvement which should inform any price cap resetting?

o   How best can the intrusiveness of the information-getting process be reduced?

5

PROMOTING ENTRY INTO REGULATED INDUSTRIES

Sir Bryan Carsberg
Director General, OFTEL

I HAVE AGREED to speak tonight about the promotion of market entry. I shall concentrate on telecommunications because that is where my experience lies. Nevertheless, I think that what I have to say probably has a good deal of general applicability in terms of the principles concerned.

Promoting Competition

All of you who have heard me speak before know about the importance I attach to promoting competition, know that I like to say that it is perhaps the most important thing that a regulator has to try to do. Often it is important, when you have a problem in regulation, to think first about the possibility that you can reduce the problem, or perhaps eliminate it altogether, by doing something in the area of assisting and promoting competition. I believe that we are on track, in the UK, to achieving a really competitive environment in telecommunications. I believe we can now have confidence that a significant number of cable television companies are going to make an impact on the market for local telecommunications. We have competition among various technologies, in particular with radio methods competing with cable-based methods, and this holds much promise for the future. In a few years time, we shall start to see the fruits of competition in a much more dramatic way than today.

I thought I would take the opportunity of this meeting at the London Business School to discuss what seem to me to be some important issues of the moment about more detailed issues in promoting competition. They are issues that had to be considered in the Duopoly Review, the conclusions of which were announced last year.

Let me start with the basic proposition that it is desirable to allow competition without a fixed limit on the number of competitors in an industry like telecommunications. Let us think about the implications of that for a minute or two. If you simply allow competition, without doing anything more, you might take the view that the effect of that would be to create a situation in which entry would take place if it could contribute to the meeting of customer goals, and would not take place otherwise. One reason not to be satisfied with that view, for utilities, might be concern about social objectives.

Social Objectives and Entry

We do, of course, have social objectives for our telephone network in the UK, as does every other country of which I am aware. The main objective is the so-called universal service obligation, the desirability of providing service throughout the country, in urban areas and rural areas alike, at more or less uniform prices. I say 'more or less' because, under our régime, there is actually an exception to the uniformity, but it is a much smaller exception than one would find in an unregulated market. Another example of a social objective is the well-known emergency call service which is provided free of charge to the customer.

The difficulty in meeting social objectives can be illustrated in relation to the rural areas problem. If you allow competitors in without restriction, they may target the most profitable areas - the urban areas - and achieve good results there by pricing close to cost and winning customers from the dominant firm which has to charge higher prices because it is required to keep prices constant across the board. Eventually, the competitors may win so many customers that the original firm has no choice but to put up prices in the areas it has retained - the rural areas - in order to make ends meet. No doubt that would be a danger if nothing were done about it but it seems to me that if you decide that you want to serve social objectives as well as having competition, then you can do so quite satisfactorily by appropriate regulation. You first have to give obligations to the dominant firm, to meet the social objectives that you have in mind, and having done that you may have to provide for the possibility that the competitors - the new entrants - should share the cost of the social obligations in some way.

The contribution of new entrants to the cost of social objectives could take the form of an access charge - a special charge for having calls terminated over the network of the dominant firm - which is provided for in the UK, though we have not yet had to activate it, and which is used in the United States. Now that kind of arrangement might not work because the effectiveness of an access charge depends on having enough calls that cross from one network into another to collect the access charge. If you had a situation where rural customers only telephoned rural customers, and urban customers only telephoned urban customers, for example, at the extreme, you might find that you never could collect access charges and so you would not be able to meet the cost of the social obligations in that way. If that were the case, you might need some sort of general levy on turnover to meet your social obligations. But it seems to me that a levy would work and the question would be whether you valued the social objectives enough to want to pursue that course.

In any case, it is comforting to remember that the relevant cost of providing services in rural areas, of meeting these social objectives, is the incremental cost. You assume first that a profitable network exists there, of the sort that would be established on purely commercial grounds, and then ask how much extra it costs to meet the extra obligations. This cost is not the sort of number that you get by the elaborate accounting exercise of allocating costs right, left and centre. A very interesting study, undertaken in Australia, shows it is a complex matter to estimate the relevant cost but the actual number is surprisingly low. I concluded that, in the circumstances of the UK, the access charge arrangement may be imperfect in principle but is likely to be sufficient in practice to support the provision of rural services, at least for some considerable period of time.

I would add another point on the subject of the desirability of allowing competition. Given that the UK started with the policy of allowing just one new entrant to challenge BT's position in operating cable-based networks, it was important that number two should face challenge as well. It is important that the challenger to BT should not feel that it has a protected position because, of course, competition between duopolists is not the most energetic form of competition imaginable and it is important for efficiency objectives that the duopolists should face challenges. This line of thought points in the direction of observing that the important question is not really about whether you allow competition; it is about whether you assist competition, whether you do something to help new entrants into the market-place. I think it is fair to say that it was a shortcoming of the formal regulatory framework that it did not face up to the problem of entry assistance. The rules do not recognise that entry assistance might be a good thing and do not set parameters for it. I was given the duty of promoting competition, a duty I take very seriously, but that was a very general expression in the Act and it was not in any way elaborated or explained; indeed, the details of the licence rules suggest that the possibility of some sort of entry assistance had not really been foreseen.

Entry Assistance

The case for entry assistance must be essentially that it serves the objective of bringing about more efficiency and variety in provision of services and does so in a stronger and more effective way than can be achieved by other means. On the other hand, there is undoubtedly, through competition, some duplication of resources resulting in a loss of certain economies of scale, that pushes in the other direction. Those differences affect the overall costs and, clearly, what one should be looking for is a system that brings about lowest cost of provision overall. Of course, there may be other benefits from competition, for example, a greater stimulus to the provision of services, and I should not forget to mention the importance of choice per se. Customers may actually feel a benefit from being able to exercise choice and that may be something to which they attach a value quite apart from, and over and above, the efficiency effects of the competition.

The methods by which one can give entry assistance include such things as allowing new entrants a choice of location. If one is constraining the pricing flexibility of the dominant company and then allowing others to choose location, that choice of location is an advantage. Another example is exclusion of the dominant company from certain areas of operation. British Telecom has been excluded under its main licence from delivering television services to customers and from providing mobile services. Importantly and interestingly, entry assistance can also be given through the pricing of the inter-connection arrangements, which any new entrant needs, with the network of the originally dominant operator.

Because of the particular balance of prices that we constrain BT to charge, the situation is that, at present, BT has to price its calls above the incremental cost of providing those calls in order to make a satisfactory rate of return overall: its standing charges do not cover the non-usage-sensitive costs of the network. That means that if, for example, Mercury collects a telephone call which it passes into BT's network for delivery by BT, and if Mercury were to be on a quite equal basis with BT, it also would have to provide a similar contribution to BT's non-usage-sensitive costs. If one excuses Mercury from some or all of that charge then that is a form of entry assistance, a sort of discounted interconnect pricing. The practical possibility of this sort of entry assistance depends on the particular balance of prices. We were perhaps fortunate in finding ourselves in a position to give such assistance when the régime began.

The scope for entry assistance was not defined in the initial regulations and the desirability of such definition led me as part of the duopoly review to try to make the position clearer and better established. It seems to me that if one is going to have entry assistance, there is a great deal to be said for doing it in a way that makes clear to everybody what is going on so that they can plan their behaviour accordingly.

Access Deficit Contributions

What we actually decided to do, and agreed with BT, was to establish a regulation which would give me the opportunity to waive the contributions to BT's non-usage-sensitive costs (which became known as access deficit contributions) for any new entrant until they had a 10 per cent market share, subject to the constraint that BT was assured that it would receive contributions after it had lost 15 per cent of market share. The idea was to limit the extent to which this entry assistance could be given, so that it would not be carried to an excessive level, while making it clear that at least some assistance could be given.

I must say, in all honesty, that I do not find entry assistance an entirely comfortable arrangement. It would be more comfortable to have the sort of market where entry assistance was unnecessary: the decisions one makes in this area are constraining and shaping and influencing the market in a way that may not produce optimal results. There is an element of subjective judgement about what you do even though you base it very carefully on economic modelling. But it seems to me that the situation where you are starting from a 100 per cent monopoly is very different from the situation where you start with several firms coming out of the starting-gate together. Where you have a 100 per cent monopolist initially, you probably have to do something of this nature to get competition started. I hope I am right in believing that, in terms of customer benefits, the action is well justified.

Price Uniformity

I will next touch on some other issues that fall in this area of entry assistance before I turn to talk about one or two issues arising out of price control and such things. I mentioned the question of price uniformity earlier. The extent to which you insist on price uniformity for different areas and different users is another factor in determining the amount of entry assistance that you give. Price uniformity was another issue that needed to be addressed and resolved in telecommunications at the same time as we were thinking about the broader position on entry assistance that I have outlined. In particular, the question arose as to whether optional tariffs be allowed - tariffs which would be set so that they would be most likely to appeal to customers who make large volumes of telephone calls. These are the customers who provide the largest contribution towards the non-usage-sensitive costs. Allowing optional tariffs is in effect allowing a rebalancing of prices - it has the property that it limits the amount of entry assistance you can give through the pricing of interconnection and has benefits in terms of encouraging use of the network by large users. Because of these factors, I decided that it would be desirable to allow BT progressively greater freedom to introduce optional tariffs, although I felt that there should be limitations in that the freedom should be phased in over a number of years. Five years is what we agreed eventually so that others in the market would have the time progressively to adjust to the effects.

Equal Access

Another issue that needs to be considered in relation to promoting entry is the question of equal access, which essentially means allowing customers to choose between various long-distance carriers in any easy way. You may have an exchange line from BT, but you can have your long-distance segment carried either by BT or Mercury, perhaps by dialling different initial numbers at the start of a long-distance number - a different number for each carrier - or you may have the option of choosing that one distance carrier or the other will carry all of your calls. Such arrangements, it seems to me, provide a useful form of competition. They differ from the actual situation as we find it. In most cases, Mercury's customers, if they have access to Mercury over BT's lines, have unequal access because they have to dial extra numbers and experience other inconveniences. Equal access would greatly facilitate long-distance competition. It is a form of help for competition that focusses particularly on long-distance rather than local competition and that may be a reason for less than whole-hearted support. I do want to encourage long-distance competition but I also want to encourage local competition. Modelling work and analysis makes me feel that the case for local competition is pretty much as strong as the case for long-distance competition in general. It varies from area to area, according to the particular circumstances, but a system of equal access might introduce undesirable bias between local and long-distance competition. To avoid or limit such bias, I decided not to give entry assistance by waiving access deficit contributions for calls that were subject to equal access.

Number Portability

Let me also mention shortly one other issue that is actually very important but I think can be briefly stated in relation to the general area of encouraging entry. This is number portability. One thing that becomes very clear, as one see firms struggling to make a success of market entry and dealing with the practical difficulties of it, is that there are many customers who are reluctant to change their numbers. If changing telephone network means changing their number, they are less likely to be willing to do so. They may change if they make enough telephone calls and they may take some lines from the new entrant and use them for outgoing calls while keeping their original lines for receiving incoming calls on the original number. That is a help for entry but it is not ideal competition in the long term. The only way to get a satisfactory outcome is to say that customers can change their telephone network without changing their telephone number. It seems that this is technologically feasible and probably, though we need to do more work on this, not prohibitively expensive. We are conducting studies at present to try to bring number portability about in the interest of a more even competitive régime.

Price Controls and Entry

Let me now turn to some aspects of price control and their interaction with the promotion of entry. I will not discuss price control generally. However, I do think that there are some very interesting issues in the interrelationship between price control and the promotion of entry and I certainly should not neglect those issues, in making price control decisions. If one were dealing with, so to speak, a straight-forward monopoly situation where you have no reasonable prospect of introducing competition, I think you should approach the broad part of price control by setting a price cap of the 'RPI minus X' sort. I think you would set it on the basis of estimates of results for a number of future years and set 'X' at a level which would produce an expectation of a rate of return of a reasonable level, a rate of return about equal to the cost of capital of the company you are regulating. However, if you are in a competitive environment, other considerations need to be taken into account.

Cost of Capital and Rates of Return

The first problem is that the cost of capital for a new entrant may actually be higher than the cost of capital for the original monopolist, and if you wish to encourage the entrant you need to set prices for the monopolist to encourage the entrant to believe that it can make satisfactory profits on the basis of its cost of capital. Quite apart from that, there needs to be a bit of a margin to attract people to what is a very difficult area of operation. Therefore a prospective return just equal to the cost of capital may not be enough. Of course, the entry assistance that I have been talking about helps by pulling the other way and the more you have that in compensation the less price control is a problem, but it is nevertheless something that has to be considered.

Another difficulty with price control is that the results of a price cap tend to be judged on the basis of traditional accounting which measures assets at their original cost, whereas new entrants have to invest at current prices in order to commence operations. And in a business like telecommunications, where some of the assets have a very long life, the difference between current and historical prices can produce a material distortion. If one sets prices high enough to allow a reasonable rate of return on current prices for the original company, then public opinion may turn against the whole process of regulation and privatisation, because of the seemingly high profits on an historical cost basis.

Price Rebalancing

Next there is the matter of price re-balancing. You might approach the analysis by looking at the elasticity of demand for calls relative to that for membership of the network and on the basis of that perhaps try to serve some concept of overall maximisation of the value of the network, marking incremental costs up more highly where the elasticities are lowest. In other words, you might adopt a Ramsey pricing approach and in plainer words you would be trying to weigh the encouragement of use of the network once people have joined it, against the encouragement of membership of the network, taking into account the extent to which higher prices put people off. However, where you wish to encourage new entry, you have to consider the extent to which changing the balance of prices will relatively encourage long-distance competition, or local competition, or competition in different areas, and allow for that in your analysis. You also need to consider the extent to which relative encouragement can be modified by access charges and discounts on interconnection pricing.

With regard to re-balancing, you feel much more comfortable about allowing increases in local prices if you know you have a strong competitor to test the prices that are charged at the local level, and be reasonably assured that high costs through inefficiency cannot be passed on to customers. But, at the same time, you are not very likely to attract that local competitor if prices are not high enough to be encouraging to entrants. Again, one has a difficult balance to strike. You might think that you could help new entrants by giving them access charges for calls that are terminated on their local networks. The problem with that is that, given the lack of number portability, new entrants do not receive so many calls into their networks as their customers make out of their networks, so access charges do not help very much.

Transparency

Finally, let me say a word or two about openness and reassurance to people about what the competitive terms really are. It has become clear recently, very largely as a result of the new situation following the Duopoly Review, that the need for transparency has increased sharply. There are many prospective entrants, but they lack information about the prospects that face them, they lack information about what is happening in different parts of the market, and they lack information about the kind of contract they could expect to get for interconnection if they were to enter. And in practice I think that lack of information can be a very important deterrent to entry. It can create unnecessary uncertainty. Because of my concern about this area I have been thinking about ways of providing a better openness and better assurance of evenness in the present situation.

Accounting Separation

It seems to me - and this has been urged on me strongly by many people - that it is now inevitable that there is an accounting separation of BT's operations. This could entail separating out local operations from long-distance operations or something like that. I am not yet quite sure in my mind where the best point of separation is. The distinction between local calls and long-distance calls is not necessarily clear-cut. It is arbitrary to some extent and I feel the need for more work to be done before I can decide the matter. However, I do think that there should be some separation along these lines and then the separated parts of BT's business should have an interconnect contract with each other, just the same sort of interconnect contract that others have with the different parts of BT, and that the terms of the BT contract should be public knowledge. This would establish a kind of bench mark which would be available to inform new entrants. It is not, I think, necessarily the case that everybody has to have the same terms, but the information about the pivotal contract should be available. Because I am talking about accounting separation and not legal separation, some information about costing arrangements is necessary to give firmness to the arrangements and generate confidence in them. And then you have to have a rule that cross-subsidisation of an unfair kind must not take place between the various parts of BT's business. Oftel is working on the firming up of our thinking in that area.

You will be clear from what I have said that we are dealing with a complex area where there are many variables which have to be settled consistently. It is not the sort of problem where you can make broad judgements and expect them to work. One needs to undertake rather detailed modelling of the markets and the major firms to understand what the effect of various detailed arrangements is likely to be. We have done, and are doing, that kind of modelling and that, I hope, will give assurance that our arrangements for promoting competition are fair and effective.

PROMOTING ENTRY INTO REGULATED INDUSTRIES

DISCUSSANT:
Professor Colin Robinson
Editorial Director, Institute of Economic Affairs

MY PURPOSE IS to place the discussion about entry stimulation in context by considering the relative roles of regulation and competition in the privatised utilities and commenting on the wide scope of British regulation.

Why Did the Privatisation Schemes Not Introduce Competition From the Beginning?

Public choice theory suggests that the programme of privatising major utilities (beginning with BT in 1984) was driven primarily by political and bureaucratic self-interest and heavily influenced by producer pressure groups.

Politicians - whatever their ideological persuasions - probably have little interest in stimulating competition. They see political benefits in raising revenues (so that spending can be increased and taxes or borrowing reduced) and widening share ownership. The gains are realised in terms of increased votes from grateful taxpayers, beneficiaries of spending programmes and lower interest rates and shareholders who received their shares at a discount. In general, such gains can best be obtained by monopoly forms of privatisation which introduce only the minimum degree of competition consistent with political ideology. Support comes from pressure groups such as the management of the utility concerned (which wants to retain market power), its unions (which expect greater rewards under monopoly) and the City (which finds the sale of monopolies easier and more lucrative than the sale of competing companies).

Thus, in terms of positive public choice theory, privatisation of utilities in a form which leaves them considerable market power is predictable. At the time of privatisation there appears to be no constituency for market liberalisation.

The Regulator as Retriever of Benefits for Consumers

Another predictable - though perhaps less obvious - result arises because, after the initial privatisation scheme, the nature of the pressures on government changes. By this time, the coalition of producer interests has fallen apart because its members have realised the gains they were seeking. But new pressures arise from disappointed consumers who complain that they have failed to benefit from privatisation.

Consumers generally are unorganised and appear incapable of delivering large numbers of votes, so their interests are under-represented in political decision-making. But large industrial consumers are well organised, powerful and vocal: in the case of gas and telecommunications they were very important forces pressing for market liberalisation. By this stage, the politicians can conveniently stand back and leave the regulator to try to accomplish what they failed to do - introduce significant competition into the industry. In that way, government can realise the political benefits of the initial privatisation and subsequently claim credit for any gains to consumers which the regulator manages to achieve - yet any upheaval of the sort which normally accompanies liberalisation of markets long monopolised will, with luck, be blamed on the regulator. If it works, it is a near-ideal political solution!

The Failure to Isolate Natural Monopolies

If I had to select one major failure in privatisation which stems from the unsatisfactory process just described, it would be the failure to isolate the 'natural monopoly' element in the industry concerned (assuming there to be some such element, given existing technology) and to regulate only that. Since the privatisation programme per se led to little market liberalisation, regulation covers almost as wide an area as it did under nationalisation (which is a different form of regulation). Because the privatised utilities have considerable market power, virtually all their activities are regulated. Thus the regulators cannot concentrate their efforts on protecting the captive consumers of 'natural' monopolies; those efforts are dissipated in attempts to supervise too many powerful organisations. In electricity, for example, the regulator is being drawn increasingly into regulating the generators, though generation is clearly not naturally monopolistic.

The wide scope of regulation is most unfortunate because it is always and everywhere an unsatisfactory substitute for competition. If competition is a process which continually discovers new knowledge and induces people to find new ways of doing things, its results cannot be simulated by regulatory devices, whether marginal cost pricing or whatever. The regulator does not know what a market outcome would have been because there has been no market process.

The Importance of Pro-Competition Regulation

In these circumstances, the competition-promoting duty imposed on most British regulators seems to me of great importance. Government failure has led to illiberal privatisation schemes. We need the regulators to make sure there are some gains for consumers. Without the duty to promote competition, there would probably still be no competition in the gas market; Bryan would have found British Telecom an even more difficult target; and electricity regulation would have been even nearer to the impossible than it is now.

Because regulation of the traditional variety - price and/or rate of return control and setting standards - is so unsatisfactory, I see the future of privatised utility regulation in terms of pro-competition regulation which stimulates entry. Administering RPI-X+Y may be fascinating, as may be resolution of the endless disputes which occur in the privatised utilities. But what is most required, as Bryan has emphasised, is entry by organisations independent of those already in the market with new ideas about production, marketing and other functions. Then the discovery process of competition will be able to work. One of the main differences between the privatised utility markets and their nationalised predecessors is that entry to those markets is possible instead of impossible. Nevertheless, entry is generally difficult and it needs to be made less so.

The public choice analyst will now see another problem. In effect, I am asking the regulators to promote entry to such an extent that they will shrink their own Offices. Indeed, they may wither away if technological change removes any natural monopolies which may now exist. Is it too much to expect? I hope Bryan will bear the problem in mind in his new rôle at the Office of Fair Trading.

6

CAN REGULATION SHAPE TECHNOLOGICAL INNOVATION?

Dr David Fisk
Chief Scientist, Department of the Environment

Introduction

THE UNDERLYING LOGIC of my thesis can be simply put. Necessity is the mother of invention. Regulations generate new necessities. Hence regulation invokes innovation. In some areas of regulatory practice the prospect of industrial innovation is a main determinant of policy. I would like to concentrate on one particular area, environmental control regulation, where the rôle of technical innovation has not been so prominent in public discussion. It turns out to have a fascinating interplay between the regulatory process and innovation. I will look at it first from the point of view of a firm looking for a competitive strategy through innovation. Then I will turn to the regulator's point of view.

I will start by challenging the traditional view of tightening of environmental regulation as one of burden, lost opportunity and lost competitiveness. First, I will argue that at the single firm level that proposition cannot be true for all firms. Indeed, I will show that for some individual firms, an aggressive environmental innovation policy offers a major competitive strategy. I will point to specific firms which, by accident or design, appear to have gained such a market advantage. Yet if this is true, then why do not more firms undertake aggressive innovation strategies to minimise their environmental impact? I will argue that the answer may lie in the form of the legislative framework within which environmental policy operates. This takes me to the regulator's point of view.

I want to look at a number of different environmental regulatory frameworks and show how they hamper or hinder an aggressive innovation policy. In particular, I want to look at how the new framework of the Environmental Protection Act (EPA) meets many of the criticisms of innovation theory. I hope to show that even the most modern legislation has a limit to the degree that it can induce innovation. That leaves us with the challenge of what other regulatory approach might be invoked.

Competitive Advantage - the Theory

Let me first show from a very theoretical point of view how environmental regulation can be used to competitive advantage. To do so I will use the model of the short-run behaviour of a firm in a very competitive market. It is a very accessible abstraction. These conditions are generally unfavourable to innovative strategies, so if I can show how an aggressive environment policy works under these conditions, I may spare you the theoretical exposition for other types of more realistic market.

The firm has maximised its profit by producing up to the point that its marginal cost of production equates to the market price. Under varying market conditions it maintains this strategy as long as the market price covers the average cost of production. If the market price falls below the average cost of production it withdraws from the market. Innovation by the industrial sector can offer advantages. It can use process innovation in the short run to reduce its fixed costs, or reduce the steepness with which marginal costs rise with increased production, gaining short-run profit. Through product innovation it can push up the price consumers are prepared to pay.

An environmental regulation may require a new piece of capital equipment, increasing fixed costs. It may involve extra running costs, raising the marginal cost curve. These changes affect the whole industry sector, so the previous market price may no longer command the same volume of industrial production. However, unless we know what happens to market demand under these circumstances, we cannot conclude with certainty that an individual firm's profitability will drop.

The extreme example is where a change in regulation makes little impact on one particular firm, but has large effects on its competitors. The market price will in general rise as the industry overall needs more incentive to produce against the new adverse position. The firm in question will actually gain market share. It will always be in the interest of such a firm, which by definition has a relatively low impact on the environment, to encourage the introduction of tougher regulations on its competitors.

The market price can shift upwards for other reasons associated with environmental strategies, which parallel product innovation effects. One of the characteristics of the 1980s was the extension by the UK retail sector of its vertical quality control to the environmental qualities of products. Some sector of a firm's market might thus be willing to pay a higher price for a product with less environmental impact. Again it is in the interests of a well-positioned firm to advance its low environmental impact as a desirable property of its product.

The striking point about a firm exploiting the environmental advantage of its product is that in terms of the simple model, this looks little different from using innovation to improve relative competitiveness. In particular, I would wish to underline one similarity. It is not being different that counts, but *successfully anticipating* the market movement. There is no point reducing environmental impact through innovation unless the regulator of the purchaser takes advantage.

Competitive Advantage - the Practice

Let me now move from theory to practice. I am not of course party to the strategy that real firms have adopted in the last decade. My alternative is to show that real world environmental regulations have changed relative competitiveness between firms.

One *cause célèbre* of the 1970s was the development of low-emission engine technology in the USA. There was a difference in technical approach, exemplified at one extreme by General Motors employing stoichmetric combustion techniques and Ford using lean-burn engine techniques. A tight NO_x specification would exclude the lean-burn approach, a slack NO_x specification would leave the stoichmetric approach exposed to heavy competition from the more efficient, high performance lean-burn engine. Both companies had the technical ability in the long run

105

to meet either specification, but one was bound to lose much of the advantage of its R & D investment to date. GM won.

A second case is provided by CFCs. CFC manufacturers had for many years expressed scepticism that the volume of world CFC emission was sufficient to damage the stratospheric ozone layer. On Gribbin's analysis[1], Dupont's change in position recommending firm controls on CFCs followed closely on its belief that it could produce a substitute. If it had retained that position it would literally have cornered the global market for refrigerant. As it was, ICI followed shortly afterwards. At the present stage of industrial development ICI's production is significantly ahead of its competitors. The R & D costs to reach this leading position were very large, and, of course, I can hardly guess whether the current lead enables them to be recouped.

A third example is the control of acid emissions from combustion plant. In effect new controls under the EC Large Combustion Plant Directive or the US Clean Air Act add a burden on coal combustion. In the UK there has been a marked increase in planned gas burn for power generation. British Gas have not missed the opportunity to draw our attention to the environmental quality of their product.

A fourth example is the introduction of unleaded petrol. This differentiated between refineries' ability to produce oxygenates, reflecting in part the refinery's vintage. Since most European governments have encouraged its uptake by price differentials it has also differentiated between those cars able to run on the new fuel and older model types that needed lead additives. In the UK the relative aggressiveness with which oil companies promoted the fuel in the early days reflected in part their capacity to produce the new fuel in quantity, Esso leading an early campaign, and BP introducing premium unleaded.

Apart from changing relative competitiveness, environmental regulations can also be an effective barrier to new entrants. The tests required of a new pesticide will typically cost £1-2 million and take several years to complete. Testing a motor vehicle for its emissions under the standard test cycle requires dedicated and very expensive test facilities. In both cases the regulatory structure actually limits the threat of small new entrants to the major players.

Rôle of the Regulator

So why do not more firms aggressively market environmental advantage? What I would now like to show is how different regulatory structures have quite profound and different effects on the opportunity to deploy an aggressive environmental strategy. It is useful to divide regulatory controls into two classes. Some controls address requirements on technology, others address requirements to be met on the environmental quality criterion.

I would like to look first at technology-based control. Measured against the criterion of innovation theory there are many things a regulator can get wrong. He can, for example, define once and for all the emission rates for a permitted process. This gives no incentive to innovate at all, except to meet the same limit at ever-diminishing cost. The regulator could thus end up with a 1930s standard of industrial environment, at much less than 1930s relative cost to the industry. As another example, the regulator could differentiate between new and existing stock of equipment in a way that discouraged new investment and encouraged patch-and-make-do in the existing stock.

The first problem is usually addressed by making the duty on the firm dynamic. 'Best practicable means' or 'best available technology' are laid as a continuous requirement, so that as soon as better technology becomes available it supersedes the older technology with the force of law. Strictly speaking, when the legislation is structured in this fashion, the regulator has little room for discretion. He becomes the prisoner of the innovatory process he has invoked. This may not resolve the problem of balance of regulatory burden between different vintages of stock.

Innovation and Vintage Stock

Suppose an industrial sector is losing out to more competitive foreign firms and has failed to win a case for some form of special treatment from its sponsoring Department. It can pursue its special pleading again by resisting the updating of the environmental standards it has to meet. If its advocacy pays off, the sector can ensure that it is only the other expanding industrial sectors that have to meet the burden of modern environmental standards.

However, it is possible to turn this argument about vintage stock on its head. Some countries abroad appear to have done just that. Environmental regulations are an instrument that Governments have at their disposal to force new investment, and, if they have it in mind, to ease out firms that have poor profitability and low capital investment records. For example, writing of Germany's acid-rain policy, Sonja Bohemar Christiansen says[2]:

> 'The limited number of macro-economic instruments available to the Federal Government ensured that stimulation of environmental investment through regulation was accepted, in the early 1980s, as an investment opportunity.'

Michael Porter of the Harvard Business School made a similar observation in *Scientific American*[3].

Innovation Beyond Regulation

There are other difficulties. Given what we know about the time necessary to establish an invention as a workable product, how does new technology ever become 'available' in the meaning of a legislative instrument? One possibility is that the next innovative step in the development is incremental on existing abatement technology. Incremental development carries with it much more confidence that it will work. Alternatively, the technology could be an import from some other country where, for one reason or another, higher standards are already required and have brought forward new solutions. This could certainly introduce step-change technology, but by definition hardly encourages domestic innovation. Both trends are discernible in the application of UK technology-based controls in the 1970s.

If the new technology merely enables the meeting of existing standards more efficiently, then its market is the well-defined group of firms that need to meet the standard. However, there is a problem in establishing the viability of a completely new technology in its earliest development phase if it does not meet this condition. If it is more effective at reducing environmental impact 'bang-for-buck', but is unfortunately also more expensive, it requires the regulator to shift the standard before any market is created. Yet the regulator is usually constrained by his statutory basis to require only *available* technology. A chicken-and-egg situation is created.

Environmental Quality Standards and Innovation

Let me now turn to a second type of regulation. It is one phrased in terms of an environmental quality standard. River quality objectives under the 1988 Water Act are an example. Discharges are permitted into the environment provided that the quality standard is not breached. Looked at from one point of view this encourages no innovation at all. Indeed, a firm may even increase its environmental impact if there is headroom left below the standard. On the other hand, once the quality standard is met, it is only by innovation that a firm can expand its production, or a new firm can operate at the site.

The greatest difficulty with the quality standard is when it is imposed under conditions where it is already breached. This applied to the air quality standards applied in US cities. As the regulator tries to crank emissions down there are a host of pressures on the marginal cost curve of firms. Sharing out emissions between firms within the umbrella of a quality standard involves the regulator in shaping innovative responses. For example, 'grand-fathering' of emissions enables old vintage stock to have a financial advantage over new entrants (and so presumably newer plant and technology) who have to 'squeeze' into the standard.

Market Mechanisms and Innovation

A third type of regulation which has received much prominence is the use of market mechanisms. At one extreme this system imposes a cost to the firm in some way reflecting its impact on the environment. This may be through the definition of liability. Strict liability for waste disposal in the USA, for example, has pushed up the price the waste disposer is prepared to pay for disposal wastes in order to ensure safe disposal and small liability. It might encourage innovative approaches to reducing production of difficult wastes, but it might discourage taking risks on innovative means of disposal. Other market mechanism approaches are more explicit levies on discharges, which may encourage innovation to reduce costs, but presumably only if the costs are large enough to command managerial attention. A third system is to address the allocation problem of emissions within a quality objective by allowing firms to trade their emissions within a group total consistent with the environmental objective. Providing there is a market in the permits it could encourage a firm to innovate to reduce its impact, and so raise cash from permit sales. Of course, if there are permits going spare then the innovation incentive ceases. There is a rapidly growing literature and experience on the use of market mechanisms. This largely concerns the efficient allocation of existing abatement technologies. It will be important as this approach develops to reflect the lessons learnt about markets and innovation.

I would like to recap the argument so far. It is easy to show that under some conditions, changes in the environmental regulations may favour an individual firm. However, the ability of the firm to exploit this advantage depends on the legislative constraints on the regulator. Different regulatory constraints offer different opportunities. Now the argument this far has focussed on the single firm well placed to take advantage through innovation. Why should the drafter of legislation, whose main task is to protect the environment in a cost-effective fashion, be concerned with the innovation process at all?

Innovation as an Environmental Imperative

There now seems no challenge to the principle that environmental quality shows the same property as most other 'superior' goods. The richer we are, the more we demand. Pearce *et al.*[4] give a convincing argument. It also seems perfectly rational. If, on becoming richer, I prefer to drink better quality wine, it surely is not surprising that I would wish to drink better quality water. If, on becoming richer, I spend more on medical care and health foods, it is surely not surprising that I would wish to have better air quality. Depending on the exact nature of a regulatory framework, it would seem that against any background of economic growth, as soon as a regulatory level is set it is out of date. There may have been a belief in the UK in the past that regulations were one-off bargains. Quite the reverse.

Rising demand for environmental quality is not the only pressure on the regulator. Suppose economic growth were only through capital growth and not technical progress. We would get richer, and our adverse environmental impact would actually increase roughly in proportion to our new income. For example, we would buy more cars, but they would all retain Morris Marina engine technology. Vehicle emissions would grow in proportion to fleet size. The gap between regulation and the desired balance would ever widen, and like any other limits-to-growth argument, eventually the growth ceases to happen.

If we now add technical progress back into the argument, we have a way to resolve the issue. The Morris Marina becomes the catalyst Rover. Even with car fleet growth, annual emissions remain constant or fall. It is sometimes argued that nations need economic growth to be able to afford environmental protection. It is the technical growth element of the economy that rescues this proposition from inconsistency.

At the day-to-day level, the importance of innovation also emerges when existing technology is already in breach of environmental objectives. It is one thing to remove lead from paint, but another to do so and have no drying agent in paint at all. It is one thing to remove lead from petrol, but another to revert to 1–star gasoline, and so on. Technical innovation is an important facilitator of environment policy. It follows that environment policy should be very much concerned with innovation, probably more than it has acknowledged in the past.

The Environmental Protection Act

The Environmental Protection Act is the most modern piece of legislation on the European statute book. I would now like to look at how well it measures up as an initiator of innovation. My main aim is to test out my previous arguments and to show that there are real limits to the rôle of regulation in innovation.

How then does the framework of the Environmental Protection Act measure up to the need to promote environmental innovation? A major change over earlier legislation is that a regulated process becomes subject to both process controls and environmental quality controls. As we have seen, quality objectives near to breach may generate innovation as necessity is the mother of innovation. Now, however, as this new abatement solution to meeting the quality objective becomes available technology, it also becomes the duty of all other firms with that process to use it. This increases, as we have seen, the incentive for the leading firm to innovate. The second change over earlier legislation is that the process controls apply to the whole process in an integrated way. The prospect for innovations is thus extended from providing end-of-pipe abatement technology to providing whole process innovation. The market advantage for process equipment suppliers through aggressive environmental innovation thus moves up from a regulation addressing add-on equipment to abate damage in one medium (say, 5-10 per cent of the cost), to an opportunity to safeguard the market position for the whole process.

111

The integrated process control embraces discharges to the solid waste system. Under EPA90 this stream is also subject to radical new changes. This stream is already a true market mechanism with industrial waste disposal subject to costs rising from around £20 per tonne, up to £2,000 per tonne. However, the maintenance of these market prices requires effective regulatory control. The new Act aims to improve the existing system substantially. In particular it places a duty of care on the waste producer and holder. In effect it provides a market incentive to pay higher costs for waste disposal and a price incentive to innovate.

As readers of the Parliamentary record will have noted, none of these changes was introduced to stimulate innovation. Indeed, the process control criterion is explicitly 'available' technology. In this sense the legislation still does not break through the chicken-and-egg problem. Nor does it provide an explicit solution to the defence that the costs are excessive, which is critical in establishing the degree to which leading firms can use environmental regulations to push the laggards over the margin of profitability. In the real world there is a limit to what can be provided for in legislation. It must be a valid defence in law to argue that what is required by law is impossible. We cannot legislate for innovation, since by definition we do not know whether a successful innovation is forthcoming.

Legislation's Limits

Thus, while the new framework captures the best from legislative approaches, it cannot fulfil all the requirements for successful innovation. Indeed, I have hardly begun to list the ingredients that we normally expect from the innovation theory for an environment that nurtures innovation. For example, you will recall the key rôle a number of workers including Nelson have identified for the first customer[5]. But who is the customer for a tougher regulation? Certainly not the regulated. Possibly the regulator, but he does not actually own plant, and cannot commission solutions. Secondly, I have not differentiated between size of enterprise, although that is a key element in innovation theory. Should small businesses in some sense be let off - lame ducked - or should they be seen as the innovative gad-flies?

There are some options that go beyond regulation. One option for the UK is simply to let other developed countries do the hard R & D work. We could continue with incremental innovation of process control, and cash-in occasional gain from quality standards pressure. We would leave it to other countries to lead on new technologies. This is a perfectly viable strategy. The advantages of such slip-streaming are obvious, but there are disadvantages.

First, it leaves sectors of our economy open to exactly the kind of aggressive innovative strategy by other countries that I described earlier. That is certainly a problem for industry policy, particularly when the environmental regulation is set at European Community level. It is not necessarily that popular in environment policy either. The priorities derived from other countries' innovation-aggressive environment policies may not necessarily line up with UK environmental priorities.

Forcing Technology

How do other countries who would contend for a leadership rôle in environmental standards close the innovation gap? The regulator has to tempt an innovation from at least one firm. In one way or another they deploy only one approach, 'forcing standards'. The famous case was the US decision to announce vehicle emission standards ahead of a technology able to deliver them. The strategy will not work if a firm (or firms) will not break ranks with its industrial sector. In some sectors Japanese regulators hold closed meetings with individual firms on the understanding that as soon as an improvement in a standard is proposed by one it will be imposed on all. Looked at from the theory of innovation, the innovation regulation needs the famous 'first customer' in the industrial sector. Selling the argument on the aggressive environmental strategies with which I opened is therefore the key.

The European Community has also deployed this tactic by setting dated stages spreading five or so years ahead for vehicle emissions. International agreements have also begun to expound this approach. The most conventional statement is to express the agreement in terms of a ceiling on future national total emissions. Set against national economic growth, this is a signal to emitters of the pollutant that they will sometime hit the ceiling and timely innovation could win them advantage. In the context of the Long Range Transboundary Air Pollution Convention the UK published its maps of critical loads for sulphur deposition this Spring and they reappear in the last two White Papers. They identify the areas of the UK where critical loads will still be exceeded in 2005 at present rates of sulphur emissions. The implications have not escaped the electricity and coal industries.

Technology forcing is more explicit in international agreements to which the UK is party than in domestic policy. That is not too surprising. As with the single firm, innovative standards are expensive if they do not correctly anticipate the regulatory régime that competitors will follow. The 1990 London revision of the Montreal Protocol process provides that the current generation of CFC substitutes would be phased out by 2040 at the latest. This is with no substitute in sight. You will see from the industrial literature that the race for that particular Holy Grail is already on in deadly earnest. The scale of world market that could be captured by 2040 by a successful substitute is almost inconceivable in scale - the refrigerant to service the requirements of 8 billion people.

A new feature of the authorisation under EPA90 also shows a version of explicit forcing. In line with the Air Framework Directive, authorisations provide a strategy for bringing the emissions of existing plant up to new plant standards within a certain time-frame. To this is added the possibility that the Secretary of State may make national plans of abatement. In effect, if plant is not to be scrapped as part of the emissions strategy, innovative solutions are going to have to be required. An element of implicit forcing is found in the DoE component of the Environmental Technology Innovation Scheme in which we part fund only those projects which promote the *tightening* of standards. The DoE's priority areas thus indicate areas where in the regulator's view standards are in need of tightening.

Finally, the White Paper introduced for the first time a whole set of indicative goals, for example on recycling, and future air quality which themselves can be re-interpreted in a forcing context. You will find those goals restated and expanded in the later anniversary document.

New Environmental Challenges

Two current issues bear on innovation and regulation. The first is defining the correct treatment of an emerging technology. The second places the question of inducing innovation central to the development of environmental policy on a global scale.

The new biotechnology is one of the first industries to be born within a regulatory framework. This contrasts with all our earlier practice, dating back to the 19th century, of regulating after a disaster has occurred. If you wish to be bloody-minded, the new technology can produce organisms which, when released into the environment, would cause absolute devastation. On the other hand, other uses of the technology should be just as safe as traditional, if more laborious, breeding methods. How should the regulations under the Act give competitive advantage to those who devise ways of enhancing rather than imperilling the environment? The primary legislative cover in EPA90 is totally inclusive, although through regulations the degree of control can be modified to reflect the *prima face* risk posed. The Act already imposes a best-available technology requirement on containment, and usually does not absolve the user of the technology from the liability of clean-up if something goes wrong. It is certainly true that the complexion of consents that have been sought to date - showing a conspicuous absence of micro-organism releases - does not reflect the early expectations from the technology. Is this innovation suppression, as some would claim, or environmental regulation moulding innovation paths?

The second issue is the encouragement of innovation to control greenhouse gas emissions. The concentration of greenhouse gases is now higher by a significant margin than the level that was attained in the last 160,000 years. We expect, on the basis of projected economic and population growth, that this figure will increase further. We know the infra-red property of these gases and can estimate the effective surface heating they will induce. Since we are already at the peak of one of the warmest inter-glacials, whatever conclusions we make about the consequences for climate, we are having to resort to difficult extrapolations of the behaviour of a climate system we do not fully understand. Governments are about to sign a framework climate convention on a precautionary basis.

The problem for the regulator and innovation theory is just how would the world decouple its growth from fossil fuel consumption. Much of the debate that is raging in many developed countries about CO2 targets is about rates of take-up of innovation. The difference in view contained in the National Academy of Science report[6] is not on the technical impact of energy conservation and fuel switching, but on the rate at which that technical impact can be taken up. This reads through to the recent announcement on the climate change issued by the US Administration, which goes so far as to give a table of expected penetration rates against the various greenhouse gas abatement measures it proposes. If the world's temperatures continue to climb - and by the end of this decade the graph of temperatures could look very convincing that something is happening - what should Governments, developed and developing, do to bring in innovation fast enough and in an optimal fashion? You will have seen that the EEC have proposed a carbon tax. Will that induce innovation or are taxes viewed by innovators as too prone to change to be worthy of long-term innovative investment?

Even this discussion is associated only with meeting goals at 2000. If climate change becomes a global problem thereafter then dramatic new innovations will be required. Are regulators courageous enough to set further goals on the assumption that this innovation will happen?

Conclusion

I hope I have shown that environmental regulations cannot impact on the individual firms in an industrial sector in a uniform fashion. They inevitably confer relative advantage. It followed that for some firms an aggressive policy on environmental innovation was profitable. Its success depended in part on the regulatory structure. Although the impact on innovation had not often figured in drawing up those regulations, different regulatory structures had very different impacts on the incentive to innovate. I also showed that the constraint of good law limited the degree to which regulation alone could promote innovation. The solutions were either to mimic advanced regulations by others or to introduce some form of forcing standards approach. The latter approach required at least one firm to break ranks. The more a country was able to anticipate the drift of competitors' regulations, the less costly forcing regulations were. They are now a common occurrence in regional environment agreements. The question I pose is whether the existing systems are still good enough to cope with the major environmental threats that are posed.

What is clear is that environmental regulation policy needs innovation. Of all the many changes in environment policy that have occurred over the last two decades, it is difficult to find any that were not enabled by technology. When it comes to the final push we would all rather do something different than simply stop doing anything. Dare the environmental regulator try and shape innovation?

The views in this paper are those of the author and do not necessarily reflect those of the Department of the Environment.

REFERENCES

1. Gribbin, J., *The Hole in the Sky*, Corgi, 1988, p.137.

2. Christiansen, S.B., and Skea, J., *Acid Rain Politics*, Belhaven, 1991, p.127.

3. Porter, M., *Scientific American*, August 1989.

4. Pearce, D.W., Markandya, A., and Barbier, E.B., *Blueprint for a Green Economy*, London: Earthscan, 1989.

5. Nelson, R.R., *et al.*, *Technology, Economic Growth and Public Policy*, Washington DC: Brookings Institution.

6. National Academy of Sciences, *Policy Implications of Greenhouse Warming*, National Academy Press, 1991.

7

NEW DEVELOPMENTS IN ELECTRICITY REGULATION

Professor S.C. Littlechild

Director General of Electricity Supply (OFFER)

Introduction

THE MAIN THEME of my talk this evening will be competition in the electricity industry and new developments in its regulation. For simplicity, this paper will concentrate on the electricity industry in England and Wales.

The electricity privatisation reflected a philosophy of competition. It differed from other privatisations (except buses) in that it was preceded by a restructuring of the industry in order to create competition. Competition was introduced in both generation and supply. The National Grid Company and 12 Regional Electricity Companies (RECs) were required to offer terms for the use of their transmission and distribution systems. A structure for trading electricity, together with a mechanism for scheduling power stations to meet demand over the transmission system, was set up by forming the electricity Pool. Three major generating companies (National Power, PowerGen and Nuclear Electric) were created out of the old Central Electricity Generating Board (CEGB), along with the separate National Grid Company (NGC). New entrants were able to enter the generation market from the outset. A timetable was established for introducing competition in the supply of electricity, purchased from the generators and sold to final users. By 1998, all

119

customers will have the right to choose their electricity supplier. The Secretary of State and the Director General were given a duty to promote competition, a duty less qualified than in other privatised utilities.

At first, there was considerable scepticism as to whether the new system would work at all. Some commentators feared that electricity supply would be disrupted because it was simply not possible to create a competitive market under which different companies generated and supplied electricity. Others worried that security of supply in the longer term would be threatened, because there were insufficient incentives for existing generators to build new plant or for new generators to enter the market. In fact, these worries have so far proved unfounded. Quite different concerns are now expressed, about how the market is working. Some are perhaps worried about the threat which they believe competition poses for their past and present positions. Others feel uncomfortable about the lack of a central plan. Yet other concerns result from frustration at the impediments to competition which still remain, and from a wish to move to a more fully competitive market more swiftly than was envisaged at vesting.

In this paper, I intend to assess the development of competition so far, to relate this to the steps I have taken to promote it, and to look at some possible issues for the future. In doing so, however, I recognise that the new system is only two years old. It is premature to draw firm conclusions at this stage about how the competitive market will work in future. Many potential competitors have plant under construction or under active consideration, but only one new entrant is actually in operation so far. Only the larger customers, representing about 30 per cent of total demand, are presently able to choose their supplier. Most electricity is still sold under three year-contracts, signed by generators and suppliers at vesting around certain expectations of how prices would or should evolve. The true test of the competitive market will come when generators, suppliers and customers can all freely negotiate, each taking their own view of the prices, risks, opportunities and threats which a competitive market offers.

The Significance of Competition

In designing arrangements to achieve the goals set out in the 1988 White Paper,[1] innovative thinking was needed. Some of the developments in

[1.] *Privatising Electricity: The Government's proposals for the privatisation of the electricity supply industry in England and Wales*, Cm.322, London: HMSO, February 1988.

competition were familiar from elsewhere. In the United States, for example, there had been a degree of competition in generation, and utilities had started to seek competitive tenders for the operation of new stations. Some third-party access to transmission systems had been negotiated. But the British system went much further, by giving any generator automatic access to the newly created wholesale market, and by giving the right to all generators and suppliers to use the transmission and distribution systems on published use of system terms.

In Britain, we also pioneered the concept of thoroughgoing competition in supply, although I now recognise that competition in supply to customers above 2MW (along with many other features of the British system) was put in place in Chile some 10 years ago.[2] Competition in supply makes a very important difference. For example, other countries have found that it is not easy to ensure that utilities which have monopoly powers over their customers operate their generation plant efficiently or run genuine competitions for the provision of generation. But if a utility knows that it has no such monopoly power over its customers, who can turn to other sources of supply if they feel that there would be a benefit to them in doing so, the pressures to operate or contract efficiently are much greater. No utility would be happy to pay more than necessary for generation if it knew that its customers were able to switch to a lower-cost rival.

The introduction of competition in both generation and supply meant that some things which had been implicit in the way the industry had previously operated now had to be made explicit, and transitional arrangements put in place to deal with them. The three main examples of this are the payments for nuclear electricity collected under the Fossil

---

[2.] The Chilean system has separate privately owned generation and distribution companies. Generation is scheduled on a merit-order basis, with cost-related rules for bidding. The distribution companies are constrained by an RPI - X type of price control, reviewed every four years. There is competition in supply to customers with maximum demand over 2MW at unconstrained prices. The prices to customers below 2MW are regulated, but cannot diverge from the unconstrained market price by more than 10 per cent. All these features of the Chilean system have worked well. The acknowledged major problem to date has been the failure to separate ownership of the transmission system from the major generating company, and the inadequately specified terms for use of the transmission system. For further information on the Chilean system, see S. Bernstein, 'The Chilean Electric Policy since the mid-Seventies', Synex Engineering Consultants, San Sebastian 2839, Santiago, Chile, circa 1991.

Fuel levy which are set to run until 1998, the three-year vesting contracts between generators and British Coal, and the matching contracts between generators and suppliers which expire in March 1993, and the arrangement which operated in the first year of privatisation to help the largest industrial customers.

We should consider what competition can and cannot achieve. It will tend to remove inherited distortions in the market: prices will tend to reflect costs more closely, whereas previously they may have been significantly above or below them. Where costs are similar there will tend to be less differentiation than before. There will also be more differentiation in prices (for example, to reflect differential costs, at different locations) where there may have been uniformity before. Investment and purchasing decisions will tend to reflect the criterion of profit rather than political criteria. Management will be under greater pressure to operate efficiently. The greater scope for choice throughout the industry, the ability to make and respond to a better deal, means that terms and contracts offered will increasingly reflect the most effective methods of producing, distributing and marketing electricity that have been discovered so far. This is the ultimate protection for customers which competition offers: the constant pressure to provide better terms than anyone else can provide.

Competition cannot be expected automatically to deliver price reductions to everyone at every time, no matter what the starting point. But I believe it is the best protection available for customers. In the absence of a market, or during a transitional period, it is never easy to judge what methods of production are the most efficient, what terms are better than others could offer. One of the most important functions of competition is to tell us.

The job of a regulator with a duty to promote competition is to encourage and facilitate competition in those markets that are potentially competitive; to identify areas of long-term monopoly where arrangements for limiting prices or ensuring terms of access need to be put in place; and to explore those borderline areas between competition and monopoly where choice can be expanded, and some elements at least of competition introduced, with a view to using market pressures more effectively to curb monopoly power.

Growth of Competition in Generation

Let me turn first to generation. In assessing progress with competition in generation, there is much that I find encouraging. Since vesting, I have issued 14 generation licences to new entrants.[3] It is not my policy to restrict either the number of licences, or the number or type of projects that licensees choose to undertake. This would not promote efficiency or be in the interests of customers. Subject to other legal constraints (for example, to protect the environment), decisions on what projects to build, when and where, and what fuel source to use are now properly for companies themselves to take.

The results of introducing competition in generation have been positive. The new projects are for the most part Combined Cycle Gas Turbine plant with a much greater fuel efficiency ratio than plant used by the major generators. There are environmental gains from lower emissions. Competition among incumbents and the prospect of entry has put great pressure on incumbent generators to increase their efficiency. Many of the new projects are underpinned by contracts with Regional Electricity Companies at prices which I understand are well below those in the initial contracts between the RECs and the major generators.

Some critics have claimed that there would be greater gains for customers if the RECs contracted instead with the major generators for power from existing coal-fired stations, at prices from British Coal which reflect the price of coal on the world market. I am sure a market exists for a significant volume of capacity from this source, and that the companies will be entering contracts accordingly. We do not yet know what will be the prices resulting from the next round of contracts, and whether they will be as low as the critics propose, but I believe they will be lower than they would have been in the absence of the spur provided by competition from the new entrants.

A market is a dynamic entity. There could well be developments in future that would change perceptions about which was the best price at which to have secured a contract. The liberalisation of the gas market, stricter environmental controls, advances in technology, changes in the

---

[3.] A list of the licences issued is contained in OFFER's list of publications, available from OFFER Library, Hagley House, Hagley Road, Birmingham B16 8QG. See also OFFER's Annual Report for 1991, available from HMSO.

dollar/sterling exchange rate - these are all factors which can, and doubtless will, change over time in ways that will affect the generation market. In recognition of this, I decided that the most sensible way to enforce the licence condition to purchase electricity economically - an obligation on the RECs in Condition 5 of their Public Electricity Supply Licences - was to examine their contracts at periodic intervals and to assess whether they represented a reasonable portfolio. By that I mean that the companies should be able to demonstrate that they have taken suitable care to assess all the options available to them, and that they have a reasonable spread of risk - not, for example, putting all their eggs in one basket either in terms of one supplier or one fuel source. I should look too for a reasonable spread of contract lengths, so that companies do not lock themselves in to the point where new and more competitive opportunities are squeezed out, as and when such opportunities arise.

I can understand the concern about the purchasing policy of the RECs when they have a price control which allows them to pass through costs into a monopoly franchise market. However, the franchise will be reduced in 1994 and abolished in 1998. I am taking steps to secure that metering arrangements enable customers in all sectors of the market to exercise effective choice of supplier.

I shall also be reviewing shortly the REC supply price control conditions. As I said in my April 1990 letter to the RECs,[4] my evaluation of economic purchasing will inform this review. If I found that Condition 5 had been breached, that would be an important factor to take into account in setting the revised price control on supply. It is also open to me to issue an Enforcement Order requiring the licensee to remedy any breach of any licence condition, with a view to protecting the interests of customers. I shall be looking for a control which provides greater incentive to economic purchasing, and to the more efficient use of electricity, than a simple pass through of costs. All the purchasing contracts which RECs sign need to be viable in a competitive market.

The examination of REC purchasing will also throw light on the issue of vertical integration between distribution and generation. A REC

[4.] The content of this letter is set out in the Prospectuses for the sale of the RECs and generators: Main Prospectus, The Regional Electricity Companies Share Offer, 21 November 1990; Main Prospectus, The Generating Companies Share Offer, 22 February 1991.

operates a distribution business as a natural monopoly, with a local monopoly over supply in its area for another six years, and the position of incumbent supplier thereafter. Is it appropriate, and if so how far, for such a company to extend back into the generation business? The possibility of 'sweetheart deals', which have occurred in other countries, is obvious. The original licences expressed reservations about this by limiting the ownership of generation to 15 per cent of a REC's market. I have the power in the licence to increase this 15 per cent limit. I have said in my April 1990 letter that I shall be looking particularly closely at purchase contracts with generation companies in which the REC has a share of ownership. My examination of the RECs' contract portfolios with respect to their economic purchasing condition should provide a useful insight into whether such ownership has been helpful and should not be resisted, or whether it is problematic and steps should be taken to restrict it.

Competition and Capacity in Generation

Another concern sometimes expressed is that competition is leading to over-capacity. Commentators draw attention to the estimates set out in NGC's latest Seven Year Statement.[5] This reported that some 24 new power stations, amounting to around 22,000 GW of capacity, had sought and obtained connection agreements with NGC. This includes new stations planned by the major generators and Sizewell B which is due to be commissioned by Nuclear Electric.

However, as NGC recognised, whether and when all the new projects proceed is another matter. Their Seven Year Statement draws together the definite information they have from companies seeking connection agreements to the grid. Such agreements are an early step in a proposed project. Some projects have yet to obtain planning permission. Others have yet to put the finance in place.

Moreover, although both the major generators have expressed an intention to close some plant at some time in the future, decisions to close particular plant are notified on a shorter time-scale - six months. So it is inevitable that some of the projections set out in the Seven Year Statement tend towards predictions of surplus capacity. In any market, one would of course expect any surplus capacity to be corrected over time.

---

5. The National Grid Company's Seven Year Statement for the years 1992/93 to 1998/99, published in March 1992.

Closure of Generation Plant

This evening is perhaps a convenient opportunity to set the record straight on my intentions in agreeing the revised licence condition with the major generators on power station closures. It is not, and never was, my intention to restrict the major generators from closing plant where there is a sound economic basis for this. Obviously, there comes a time in the life of any asset when the owner decides that the costs of maintaining and operating it exceed the revenues that can be obtained from doing so. This will depend not only on the physical state of the plant and the costs of repairing and maintaining it, but also on the estimated future revenues. A particular station might well be capable of running on for a further period, but the owner may decide that competitive pressure is driving Pool and contract prices to the point where he does not consider the return on the assets to be sufficient to keep it. This does not necessarily mean that a different owner would take the same view, either of the costs of operation or of the future course of prices.

I do not believe that it is in the long-term interests of customers artificially to keep uneconomic plant in the system, or to keep Pool prices artificially low. Rather my concern is to prevent *economic* plant being taken off the system, as a means of making Pool or contract prices artificially high. In the context of my Pool Price Inquiry, where I discovered evidence of availability declarations being used to increase Pool prices, I thought it best to take steps to ensure that closure of plant would not be used to the same end. The automatic linking of Pool price to available capacity, via the Loss of Load Probability, which was primarily intended to provide an additional incentive to build new plant, has the unfortunate consequence of providing an additional incentive to remove existing plant if you happen to be a major generator in the market. A second concern is therefore to ensure that the discipline of alternative potential ownership of closed plant is effective.

The point of the new licence condition is to provide more reassurance that decisions taken by the major generators to close or retire plant are decisions which it is reasonable for them to take, against the background of a competitive market. It will give me power to appoint an independent assessor to investigate decisions by the major generators to close plant. In providing advice to me, the independent assessor will naturally have to establish the price or prices at which third parties would wish to purchase the plant, site or associated facilities, which is what I said in the

Pool Price Inquiry Report[6] would be necessary. These third parties may well have other ideas for refurbishing the plant and reducing its operating costs.

I see this procedure as a useful reinforcement for me in understanding closure decisions and assessing whether they are within competition law. If I were to decide that a certain decision was anti-competitive - for example, that it had been taken for the purpose of withdrawing capacity from the market in order to drive up the price and produce a net gain for the company concerned on its other plant - there would be various steps that I could take, using my powers under the 1989 Electricity Act and relevant competition legislation. There is also the possibility that companies holding generation licences could apply to the Secretary of State for compulsory purchase powers. This would enable them to acquire the site under procedures set out in the Electricity Act. So my new licence condition provides an additional safeguard and one which I hope will further boost public confidence in the electricity market.

Are more steps needed to reinforce the discipline of alternative ownership? Some (including the Select Committee on Energy)[7] have suggested that the major generating companies should be forced to sell surplus plant. The proposal that a company should be required to dispose of certain assets, or that I should have the power to require it to do so, would be a major step. I do not rule it out in appropriate circumstances - for example, as a remedy to a practice or situation which the MMC has judged to be against the public interest. However, my Pool Price Inquiry Report did not find that the two major generators had in fact closed plant for anti-competitive reasons. I therefore do not believe that it is necessary or appropriate at this stage to seek such powers, although I welcome the Select Committee's support in the event that it becomes necessary to do so.

Competition in Supply

I turn now to competition in supply. As I noted earlier, it was a major innovation to introduce competition in supply. The Government decided

---

6. OFFER, *Report on Pool Price Inquiry*, December 1991.

7. House of Commons Select Committee on Energy, *Second Report: Consequences of Electricity Privatisation*, HC113-I, II, III, London: HMSO, 26 February 1992. Response from the Director General of Electricity Supply, 9 June 1992.

on a timetable for phasing it in over eight years. We are now in the third year of contracting since competition was first permitted. However, we are still at an early stage where only those customers (some 4,000 in total) who have maximum demand above 1MW can choose their supplier.

TABLE 1

SECOND-TIER SUPPLY IN ENGLAND AND WALES[1]: BY REGIONAL ELECTRICITY COMPANY 1990/91 - 1991/92

(per cent)

REC	Average percentage of the number of non-franchise sites		Average percentage of the total non-franchise demand (GWh)	
	1990-1991[2] taken by second tier supply[3]	1991-92 expected to be taken by second tier supply	1990-91 taken by second tier supply1	1991-92 expected to be taken by second tier supply
Group 1 E. Midlands Eastern Midlands Southern	19.75	26.5	31.0	31.0
Group 2 Seeboard Yorkshire London NORWEB	28.0	36.2	41.0	46.7
Group 3 South Wales Northern S. Western MANWEB	40.0	51.0	56.5	70.5

[1] These figures have been revised since the 1991 Annual Report was published.

[2] 1990-91 percentages are based on figures that have been adjusted to take into account the fact that the majority of contracts in this financial year applied only to nine months. For this reason comparisons with the 1991-92 figures must be treated with caution.

[3] Percentages calculated as simple averages of the sum of the percentages for each REC in the group.

In 1990/91, the first year of the competitive supply régime, second-tier supply - that is, supply by someone other than the REC in whose territory the customer is located - accounted for an average of 45 per cent of non-franchise electricity supply sales. There was, however, considerable regional variation - from under 31 per cent to over 56 per cent - as illustrated in Table 1.

In the next year, 1991/92, second-tier supply increased slightly, to around half of all sales in the competitive market. As before, the proportion varied considerably from one area to another, and was over 70 per cent in some areas. No doubt this variation reflected the composition of the customer base in each area, as well as the different policies adopted by the local RECs. Preliminary indications are that the overall proportion of second-tier supply remained at a similar level in 1992/93, though there were some changes for individual companies.

In general, customers who have been free to choose their supplier seem to have experienced an improvement in the standard of service. Contracts have been tailored more closely to their individual needs and they have been able to obtain advice on their electricity use. This seems broadly to have been the case whether or not customers have actually taken second-tier supply. In other words, the very *possibility* of choice has led to better terms being offered.

The Pool

Another aspect of the generation market which has received attention is that of developments in the Pool. In the Report on Pool prices which I published last year, I noted that prices had been low in the first year after vesting and had subsequently risen. I said that it was not possible to say that the then current level of prices was either too high or too low. Nevertheless, I identified several areas of concern. I have addressed these in the licence amendments which have now been agreed with the major generators, in my Report on the rôle of gas turbines, and in my forthcoming Report on constrained-on plant.[8]

The Select Committee noted a large number of criticisms of the Pool's methods and procedures, and of its effects on the market. It made several

---

[8.] OFFER, *Report on Gas Turbine Plant*, June 1992; OFFER, *Report on Constrained-on Plant*, October 1992.

recommendations for change, and posed some searching questions about the Pool's fundamental rôle.

The creation of a market for trading electricity, where none previously existed, was no easy task. The designers deserve credit for putting in place a workable mechanism in time to allow the privatisation to proceed. Pool members and the Pool Executive Committee have also devoted a great deal of time and effort to making the system work, and are themselves seeking further improvements.

I believe there is now scope for further development, consistent with many of the Select Committee's recommendations. Pool charges should be more reflective of costs. My Report on gas turbines suggests ways of making the provision and remuneration of certain Pool services more responsive to market forces. In general, the Pool should be a means of facilitating competition, and improving the options open to customers, generators and suppliers, rather than a means of imposing a strait-jacket on the development of the market.

It is important to explore the prospects for incorporating a greater rôle for the demand side of the market, as the Select Committee said. I indicated in my Pool Price Inquiry Report that there may well be scope for demand-side bidding. If properly realised, demand-side bidding can facilitate the balancing of supply and demand, increase efficiency and reduce costs, and offer profitable opportunities to customers. I am currently investigating ways in which it may be implemented. As with all amendments to the trading arrangements, practical considerations will play an important part in determining how this can be best accomplished.

I shall continue my efforts to ensure that the Pool becomes less burdensome, particularly on smaller independent generators and suppliers, and more sensitive to the needs of customers. Buying and selling through the Pool can be both costly and complicated. It might well be appropriate if potential users join the Pool only if they perceive that it is to their advantage. Suitable ways would need to be found to provide the other functions of the Pool, such as the merit order scheduling of plant and the handling of transmission losses, and the remuneration of other services presently paid for by Pool members. The Select Committee's recommendations on this issue will repay further exploration.

The Contract Market

Most customers are served through contracts rather than from purchases at Pool price. The vast bulk of contracts between generators and RECs which serve the franchise market were for a period of three years, and hence have remained unchanged since vesting. The developments in the contract market which have taken place have mainly pertained to the competitive non-franchise (above 1MW) sector, which represents about 30 per cent of the total market.

In 1990/91, the first year after vesting, contract prices available to non-franchise customers were significantly below prices obtaining before privatisation. Price reductions of the order of 15 per cent were frequently reported to us, and the Major Energy Users Council[9] (MEUC) said that a significant number of its members reported reductions in excess of 20 per cent. However, some very large customers, who had previously benefited from special arrangements to purchase electricity from the CEGB, did not experience such large reductions. In the second year, 1991/92, non-franchise customers reported prices at about the same level. In 1992/93, there were reports of significant price rises, but the actual extent of this is unclear. The MEUC talked of price rises up to 20 or 30 per cent. An unpublished questionnaire of MEUC members in April 1992 is understood to have shown price offers for 1992/93 around 15 per cent higher than prices paid in 1991/92. A survey by National Utility Services[10] found lower price increases of around 8.6 per cent.

The DTI publishes a regular survey of prices to manufacturing sites in Great Britain, which gives a more systematic picture of developments.[11] It is based on a stratified sample of over one thousand sites, weighted towards larger users. Putting the Survey data into real terms at 1990 prices, it reveals that the average price of electricity purchased by large manufacturing industry (sites using over 880 MWh per annum which will also be outside the franchise) was about 3.6p/kWh in 1989/90; it fell by about 14 per cent in 1990/91, then rose by about 2 per cent in 1991/92, but (in real terms) was still about 12 per cent below pre-vesting prices at the

---

[9] Energy Information Centre/MEUC, *Energy Privatisation, The Customers' Verdict*, June 1991.

[10] National Utility Services (NUS) Limited, Press Release, 27 May 1992.

[11] Department of Trade & Industry (DTI) survey published in the statistical bulletin *Energy Trends*, September 1992.

end of 1991/92. The average price to very large manufacturing sites (which are a subset of the above large sites, using over 150,000 MWh per annum) was about 3.0p/kWh in 1989/90; it fell by over 9 per cent in 1990/91, then rose by over 6 per cent in 1991/92 and was still (in real terms) over 3 per cent below the pre-vesting level at the end of 1991/92. Provisional figures for 1992/93 suggest that for both groups of customers, the reported average price increase in 1992/93 is only about 1 per cent in real terms (perhaps about 5 per cent nominal), which is much less than the figures quoted in the previous paragraph. The reasons for these discrepancies are as yet unclear. The DTI Survey evidence does suggest, however, that the average customer in the competitive market in fact still has lower electricity prices in real terms (about 11 per cent lower) than before privatisation. (This contrasts with the experience of small manufacturing sites in the franchise market which, according to the *Energy Trends* survey, paid higher prices in 1989/90 - about 6.1p/kWh - and whose prices have since increased in real terms by nearly 7 per cent.)

The rise in the generation contract price coincided with the auction of contracts held by Nuclear Electric at the end of 1991. I believe this had a particularly significant effect on the market at that time. Nuclear Electric's expected generation represents nearly 20 per cent of generation in England and Wales. But most National Power and PowerGen generation was tied up in the vesting contracts for the franchise market (70 per cent of the total market). Nuclear Electric's policy is likely to have had a major impact on prices obtaining in the non-franchise market (30 per cent of the total market) since it accounted for nearly two-thirds of available capacity there. The reserve price which Nuclear Electric set for the auction represented a significant increase on the contract prices available in the previous year and resulted in less than half of Nuclear Electric's expected generation being contracted. As a result of Nuclear Electric's dominant position in the market at that time, this contributed to a restriction of choice of contracts for large customers and left such customers more vulnerable. Although I took action to encourage Nuclear Electric to make more contracts available rapidly, I was disappointed at its lack of flexibility on price and the consequent limited increase in sales. I shall continue to monitor Nuclear Electric's dealings in the contract market and hope that arrangements can be put in place to make it a more effective competitor.

Although the rate of new entry by independent generators has been encouraging, it will inevitably take time to have full effect. Moreover, because of a variety of factors - for example, higher gas prices, the possible surplus of future capacity, potential difficulties in securing planning consents, and uncertainties about the extent and terms of contracts from National Power and PowerGen covering future output from their coal-fired stations - there must be some doubt as to how much more new entry there will be of this kind. The major generators are thus likely to retain a very significant share of the market for some years to come.

In order to reduce dominance in the market, the Select Committee recommended that, when the electricity market has had time to develop further, and not later than 1995, I should decide whether the two main generators should be referred to the Monopolies and Mergers Commission (MMC). In view of the factors mentioned above, I appreciate the Select Committee's concern. I therefore intend to work within that framework. But I hope that the parties concerned will consider what steps they could take to secure a more competitive generation sector without the need for such a reference.

Problems of Price Control

The prices charged for the use of the transmission and distribution systems have moved quite unevenly since vesting. Although there has been little or no price rise this year, and in several cases there have been price falls, last year saw price increases in the 15-20 per cent range. Certain customers experienced even larger increases. This erratic path stems partly from the operation of correction factors in the various price controls. It would not be appropriate here to explain the price control conditions in all their detail but I will use the following stylised examples to explain how the operation of a correction factor can contribute to price instability.

Assume that prices start at a base level which is equal to the maximum allowed by the price control conditions and that the only source of error in matching actual prices to the maximum allowed by the cap is the imperfect forecast of the RPI.

In the first example, average distribution price (REV for average revenue) in the base year starts at 1.8 p/kWh. Over a three-year period the RPI increases at a constant rate of 5 per cent a year, but price increases are based on forecasts of the RPI over the three years of 4, 6 and 5 per cent.

Table 2 illustrates the associated changes in maximum allowed revenue net of the correction factor (MAR) and in average price.

TABLE 2:
FIRST EXAMPLE: ELECTRICITY PRICES AND PRICE CONTROL

	BASE	YEAR 1	YEAR 2	YEAR 3	TOTAL
REV (P/KWH)	1.80	1.87	2.02	2.06	7.76
FORECAST RPT (%)	NA	4.0	6.0	5.0	NA
% Δ IN REV	NA	4.0	8.0	2.1	NA
MAR (P/KWH)	1.80	1.89	1.98	2.08	7.76
ACTUAL RPI (%)	NA	5.0	5.0	5.0	NA
% Δ IN MAR	NA	5.0	5.0	5.0	NA

In setting prices for year one, the RPI is estimated to increase by 4 per cent and so as a result average price is set at 1.87p. Because of the under-estimate, this is 1 per cent below what the cap will (subsequently) be, which is 1.89p.

The allowed price change in year two can be broken down into two components. First, the base level of prices can be adjusted upwards to the maximum allowed by the price cap, net of the correction factor (MAR). Since the RPI is forecast to increase by 6 per cent, and prices started from a level 1 per cent below the cap, this will allow a 7 per cent price increase. Second, there is a revenue correction to enable the amount allowed in the current year to be adjusted to recover the difference between the maximum revenue allowed in previous years, based on outturn numbers, and the revenue actually received. This retrospective adjustment is called the correction factor. In year two it allows prices to rise by an additional 1 per cent. Adding the 7 per cent increase in base prices to the 1 per cent increase due to the correction factor gives an overall allowed price rise of 8 per cent in year two, to 2.02p.

In year three the allowed price change can again be analysed in terms of the two components. First, the new forecast of RPI increase is 5 per cent. But because prices in year two were higher than otherwise because of the operation of the correction factor and the over-forecast of the RPI, the increase in prices necessary to give the maximum allowed by the cap, net of the correction factor, is 2 per cent less than the new forecast of the

RPI. Second, the year three correction factor reflects the over-forecast of the RPI in the previous year which led to an over-recovery of revenue; as a result, the price increase allowed in year three is reduced by a further 1 per cent. The net effect is an allowed price rise in year three of approximately 5-2-1 per cent = 2 per cent.

To summarise, in this example, a constant inflation rate of 5 per cent for three successive years was forecast as 4, 6 and 5 per cent. This represents only a small error in forecasting, for only two years, but the operation of the correction factor led to allowed price increases of 4, 8 and 2 per cent - a more erratic path of prices.

In practice, the errors in RPI forecasts have been much greater than in the previous illustrative example. The actual RPI profile of 10.9 and 3.7 per cent in 1990/91 and 1991/92 was typically forecast at 6 and 6 per cent. This led to significant rises (up to 20 per cent) in distribution use of system charges at the start of 1991/1992 and price falls (in real terms) at the start of 1992/1993.

The following example is typical of the price rises generated by the operation of the distribution price control. Assume actual inflation rates of 10.9, 3.7, 3.7 and 3.0 per cent, and a positive X factor of 2.5 per cent. If inflation had been correctly forecast, there would have been a 13.4 per cent allowed price increase in the first year (10.9 + 2.5 per cent) followed by allowed increases of 6.2, 6.2 and 5.5 per cent. In the event, RPI was forecast at 6.0, 6.0, 4.2 and 3.0 per cent. These errors in forecasting led to a price increase of 8.5 per cent in the first year followed by allowed increases of 17.9, -1.6 and 6.7 per cent. Again, this represents a more erratic path of prices, particularly with an increase of nearly 18 per cent followed by an actual price reduction. Table 3 summarises these calculations.

I shall be addressing this instability as well as the general level of prices charged when I review the price controls. I intend to ensure that future prices are no higher than necessary to enable the licensees to run an efficient business. This means closely scrutinising their projected capital expenditure and operating expenses. In considering what cost of capital would be plausible for them, it is necessary to take into account the relatively protected stable businesses in which each of them is engaged. The National Grid Company's price control on transmission charges is

TABLE 3:
SECOND EXAMPLE: A HYPOTHETICAL DISTRIBUTION BUSINESS (X = 2.5)

	BASE	YEAR 1	YEAR 2	YEAR 3	YEAR 4	TOTAL
REV (P/KWH)	1.80	1.95	2.30	2.27	2.42	10.74
FORECAST RPT	NA	6.0	6.0	4.2	3.0	NA
FORECAST RPI + X	NA	8.5	8.5	6.7	5.5	NA
% Δ IN REV	NA	8.5	17.9	-1.6	6.7	NA
MAR (P/KWH)	1.80	2.04	2.17	2.30	2.43	10.74
ACTUAL RPI + x	NA	13.4	6.2	6.2	5.5	NA
% Δ IN MAR	NA	13.4	6.2	6.2	5.5	NA

due for replacement on 1 April next year and I am presently reviewing this.[12] Controls on the supply and distribution prices charged by the regional electricity companies for distribution are due for replacement from 1 April 1994 and 1995 respectively, and work on them has already begun.

Some have suggested that I should accelerate the REC reviews so that new controls can be implemented earlier. I well understand the concerns of users. However, there are disadvantages as well as advantages associated with the premature review of price controls. They were set on the basis that there would be a reasonable period between reviews, giving companies the incentive to improve efficiency and reduce costs during that period. If a regulator is seen to intervene constantly in the operations of a company, there will be an adverse effect on the incentive for that company to improve its efficiency and reduce costs. What is more, the degree of regulatory risk to which it is subject may be perceived as greater. Consequently, there may well be some increase in the rate of return which investors require - that is, in the company's cost of capital - and so a higher level of prices for customers in the longer run. Taking these considerations into account, I do not believe that an earlier review of this price control is warranted at present.

Borderline Areas

There is obviously a substantial degree of monopoly in the transmission and distribution businesses and that is why there is a need for price

---

[12.] See my subsequent 'Statement on Future Control of National Grid Company Prices', 7 July 1992. This, *inter alia*, tightened the control to RPI -3, and put RPI on an historic instead of a forecast basis.

control. Nevertheless, there are possibilities of competition in some aspects, and I have been concerned to encourage the possibilities of competition where these exist. For example, on-site generation (that is, the installation of generation plant on the customer's own site) provides one form of competition. With my active encouragement, the Pool rules have been changed to ensure that own generators are charged only for their exports to or imports from the system, rather than on the basis of their gross output, and thereby are not unduly disadvantaged. This principle of 'netting off' can be carried further. The possibility of matching some electricity demand and supply locally could provide valuable competitive pressure on the costs, efficiency and terms offered by NGC transmission and REC distribution networks. I am pleased to report that NGC and some RECs are also moving in the direction of competition by allowing customers to obtain competitive quotes from other firms to provide connections to the system, or to provide the connections themselves.

Discrimination and Cross-Subsidy

In areas where competition is limited, the licence prohibitions on discrimination and cross-subsidy constitute a further protection for customers and for competition. Major generators cannot favour their own supply businesses at the expense of businesses run by others. Nor can they structure their prices so as to disadvantage would-be competitors in generation - for example by offering specially low prices to customers who would otherwise be attractive targets for a new entrant. This protection of new entrants should be in the longer-term interest of all customers. However, non-discrimination does not mean that prices must be the same to all customers. It means that differences in prices (or other terms and conditions) must reflect differences in cost. Where customers' circumstances vary and the costs of supplying them are different, then correspondingly different prices could clearly be appropriate. The volume of sales, load factors, conditions of interruptibility, location of premises, and date and duration of the agreement are all factors which may be relevant in deciding what is, or is not, legitimate discrimination.

There has been some discussion as to whether the volume of sales warrants a discount on the generation price (as opposed to lower charges for the use of the distribution system). On the factors so far put to me, it is not clear that there are savings at the power station in supplying 1 MW to one customer in any hour compared with supplying 1 KW each to a thousand customers. Large customers often have flatter load curves, and lower average prices may be warranted for that feature, but I do not at present see that there should be a difference in the generation price to different customers in a particular half-hour.

Some large customers are very concerned about the implications and effects of the non-discrimination conditions. As noted, a main purpose of these conditions was presumably to protect customers by preventing predatory behaviour which could deter or drive out competitors. This followed the MMC Report on British Gas. The non-discrimination conditions were put in the licences of the major generators only. I certainly do not consider them appropriate for smaller generators whose market position does not enable them to deter entry. There is a disapplication provision which means that the non-discrimination conditions in effect fall for review by 1995, and it will then be relevant to consider under what conditions they should or should not be renewed.

Domestic Customers and Competition

I have said little this evening about domestic customers and the franchise market. Yet I am very conscious that it is they who are presently shouldering the main burden of the previous distortions in the electricity industry, and who have most to gain from competition. I am taking steps to ensure that the benefits of competition and of energy efficiency become a reality for these customers, by the timely installation of meters appropriate to the next century rather than the last.[13] I am also pleased that the 1991 Competition and Services Act gives domestic customers as well as industrial ones the right to own their own meter by agreement with their supplier. But a full discussion of these issues would take us too far afield.

Conclusion

The electricity industry is a complex one, and introducing competition into it cannot be expected to be easy. I am only too well aware of the criticisms and concerns that have been voiced at many different aspects of the way things have developed. But I hope to have shown in this paper that competition is developing in generation and supply; that it has already produced some worthwhile benefits; and that more benefits are in prospect. Not surprisingly, there have been problems, but I believe that

[13]. OFFER, *Energy Efficiency Consultation Paper*, December 1991, and OFFER, *Metering Consultation Paper*, January 1992. Also OFFER, *Energy Efficiency: The Way Forward*, October 1992.

several of these have already been dealt with by my Office, and others are capable of being addressed by the regulatory framework. Importantly, some of the complaints should be disappearing with the growth of more effective competition.

I do not see competition as the be-all and end-all. This paper has clearly explained the need for various additional regulatory actions to protect customers fully. But I hope to have shown that competition has a central rôle to play.

8

AIRPORTS AND AIRLINE COMPETITION

The Rt. Hon. Christopher Chataway
Chairman, Civil Aviation Authority (CAA)

Introduction

I WOULD LIKE to begin by thanking you, Chairman, for the invitation to talk to you tonight. Both this and the previous series of lectures have taught us much about the common issues which regulators face - we have a lot to learn from each other - and also about the differences.

By giving me the title 'Airports and Airline Competition' you have given me the opportunity to compare the very different natures of airport and airline competition and to discuss how these are reflected in their regulation. I also want to take a lead from previous speakers and talk about some of the main issues which have arisen during the year. On the airline side these are principally developments in Europe, and the main event on the airport side has been our quinquennial review of the British Airports Authority's (BAA's) London airports.

But first a word about the Civil Aviation Authority itself. As you probably know our main tasks are to provide an air traffic control service - and this is by far the largest part of the Authority - and to regulate the UK airline and airport industries. Our regulatory rôle comprises both safety and economic regulation. I will not be discussing safety regulation tonight except to emphasise that our first consideration is and always will be for the safety of the air transport user. I should also explain that the Economic Regulation Group has other regulatory and advisory functions which would need talks of their own. As well as regulating airports and airlines we also licence tour operators through the Air Travel Organisers' Licensing system; we advise the Government on airline and airport policy matters and we publish industry statistics and surveys.

The CAA has been responsible for the economic regulation of the UK airline industry since it started work in 1972, whereas the regulation of airports is new. It was grafted on to us by the Airports Act of 1986 as a direct consequence of the Government's policy of privatising BAA, of encouraging the privatisation of airports generally, and of ensuring that where still publicly owned they acted so far as possible as stand-alone enterprises. The privatisation of telephones, electricity, gas and water required the creation of new specialist regulators, but the CAA was already in place dealing with some aspects of the airport industry as well as with airlines.

Airline Regulation

Airline regulation has a much longer history. In the early days of commercial aviation there was a general view, common to all countries and to most modes of transport, that the public interest would best be served and a viable and extensive network provided if what was seen as wasteful and destructive competition were avoided. This view was held particularly strongly in the USA, despite the vigorous free enterprise doctrine which prevailed in most other industries. The general view was that important benefits would be lost if 'cream-skimmers' were given free rein. No real conflict was seen between producers' and users' interests. Thus, far from encouraging competition, regulators saw their main rôle as preventing it from breaking out!

Between the war and the Edwards Committee report of 1968 there was gradual liberalisation. Airlines other than the state corporations were allowed to offer supplementary services so long as they did not impinge significantly on scheduled services. By the 1960s the charter industry was growing fast, despite nominally severe restrictions on their conditions of sale. By the time of Edwards opinion was beginning to switch towards the view that the airline industry was potentially much like any other competitive industry, although immediately post-Edwards there was a policy of statutory duopoly with BA seen as the main provider, BCal as the second force and other airlines in a supplementary rôle. Arguments about traffic diversion, duplication of effort and so on still had some sway and there was a fear - incongruous now - that if BA were exposed to too much competition it would die the death of a thousand cuts. There are some interesting echoes in all this of the present arrangements for competition in telecommunications.

In the UK, and indeed in Europe, the most rapid changes came in the late 1970s and the 1980s. The Civil Aviation Act of 1981 gave further emphasis to what was already becoming a reality and the onus of proof was firmly upon those who objected to an airline flying a route. British Airways, which had traditionally opposed applications by other airlines to compete directly with it, gradually relaxed its stance and by the time of its acquisition of BCal in 1987 it was arguing in public for open skies. Real opportunities for competition opened up, with more liberal agreements on some routes between the UK and Europe: those with Holland and Ireland are the most quoted examples. In 1987 the European Community adopted a package which was a major break-through, requiring governments to accept airlines licensed by other governments on most significant routes and removing their ability to insist on a close balance between the capacity offered by each country's airline. This enabled a considerable increase in services to Europe by British Airways' UK competitors.

As a final comment on developments in the 1970s and 1980s, no UK observer can resist pointing out that the USA was a relatively late convert to liberalisation. Until 1978 it had a regulatory apparatus which made the traditional European system look permissive. In particular, it took a very stern line on new entry. For example, it resisted Laker's arrival onto the North Atlantic by raising trivial technical objections - a reaction which one of my predecessors called 'unconscionable' procrastination. However, after 1978 the US adopted deregulation with all the zeal of a convert.

So what is the CAA's rôle in all this? We are the licensing authority for UK airlines. We have two main statutory objectives, which are to encourage UK airlines to provide a range of services and to further the reasonable interests of users. We are required to consult the industry and users from time to time on the policies by which we will seek to achieve these objectives. Unlike most of the other regulators who have talked to you this summer we have no direct statutory objective to promote competition, but a central plank of our policy is that competition, where it is achievable, is the best available means of meeting these objectives. Thus, once we are satisfied that the applicant is British, which is still required of us, and meets the financial provisions of the Civil Aviation Act, we grant the vast majority of licence applications. There is a statutory objection procedure - often but not always involving public hearings.

Nowadays these cases involve mainly routes where foreign governments limit the number of flights available to UK airlines, very thin routes or routes where there is a prima facie case of anti-competitive behaviour. Also a number of our hearings concern domestic services to the Channel Islands, where special factors apply. I should also add that, except for the Channel Islands, short-haul charters operate under area licences which enable them to fly from anywhere in the UK to anywhere in Europe. As a measure of the importance of charters, you may be interested to know that in 1991 UK airlines carried 21 million passengers on charters compared to just under 35 million on scheduled services.

I spoke a few moments ago about liberalisation in Europe and we are now on the threshold of very important changes. By the beginning of next year a new package will be in place dealing with airline licensing, market access and fares. The most significant of these changes in terms of our duties and powers is that national authorities will be required to grant licences so long as they meet certain, broadly liberal, criteria. We are generally happy about this, particularly since it is intended to make states which have been reluctant to licence airlines to compete with their own flag carriers, or which have confined such competition to a minor rôle, to adopt a more open approach which should be in the interests of travellers generally. One area in which we are less happy is that some activities - particularly air taxis - which we do not now regulate are to be drawn into the licensing net.

I would like to end this discussion of airline regulation and competition by raising an issue on which I have spoken on other occasions and at greater length. This is the importance of a clear and fast-acting mergers and competition policy in Europe. The history of the USA since deregulation, and to some extent that of Europe as well, shows that, for scheduled services at least, large ubiquitous well-known airlines have enormous advantages in maintaining their market strength in the face of potential, sometimes more efficient, competitors. Many of what used to be called the flag carriers have unassailable positions at their home airports, positions which are especially strong where congestion at peak times already precludes any new competitor from getting established there. There have been some encouraging instances of new entry in some markets - Gatwick/Scandinavia is an example - but at the moment the general trend in the industry is towards mergers or alliances, and potentially to less competition rather than more.

That is why I have been stressing that *laissez-faire* alone is not enough and Brussels's general and highly commendable policy of opening up markets must be accompanied by an effective mergers and competition policy. There must also be effective and rapid mechanisms to deal with anti-competitive behaviour. The notion from the early days of US deregulation that such behaviour is irrational in 'contestable' markets is now wholly discredited and people are more aware than they were of the diverse forms which such behaviour can take. I have great sympathy with the views of Sir Sydney Lipworth, the MMC's Chairman, who argued again last week that institutional change is needed if the Commission is to cope effectively with the competition issues for which it has been given responsibility. Both he and Dr Rolf Geberth of the German Federal Ministry of Economics have criticised the existing highly politicised system for dealing with competition issues and have urged that a body should be created - a European cartel office or MMC - which would have an investigatory function independent of the Commission.

My second main area of concern is that the industry's traditionally duopolistic structure remains on many routes, and is likely to persist so long as runway capacity falls short of demand at the most popular airports. Real innovation, particularly at the higher end of the fare spectrum, tends to come only when a third airline can find its way in. For that reason I believe it is important that the passenger whose needs are such that he cannot use the cheaper excursion fares on charters should continue to have some protection from blatant overcharging. I am very glad that our view on this has carried some weight in Brussels and that the architects of the new fares package now look as if they are not going to throw out the baby with the bath water in their commendable enthusiasm for liberalisation. We hope these new arrangements will work and will certainly give them our support.

Airports Regulation

Our rôle in airports regulation is much more recent, dating from the Airports Act of 1986. When telephones, electricity, gas and water were privatised the Government recognised that they had substantial monopoly power. While some of their activities were competitive, or might become so in time, the Government saw a need for specialist regulators, reinforced by the MMC, to ensure that prices were not exploitative, that dominant positions were not abused, and that competition was encouraged and facilitated.

New agencies were created for telephones, electricity, gas and water but since the CAA already existed as an airline regulator, and indeed also as the regulator of airport safety, the task of economic regulation was given to it. Our duties and powers are comparable with those of the other specialist regulators with the significant exception that, as with airline regulation, we have no direct duty to foster competition. Our main statutory duties are to further the reasonable interests of airport users, to promote the efficient, economical and profitable operation of airports, and to encourage necessary investment in time to satisfy demand. Our main tasks are to set price formulae for those airports specifically designated by the Secretary of State - at the moment these are BAA's London airports and Manchester - and to deal with complaints of exploitative, anti-competitive or exclusionary behaviour at these and two dozen other airports in the UK.

This rôle is almost unique. Private airlines are by no means unusual and privatisation is now a world-wide phenomenon, but as far as I know the UK and New Zealand are the only countries which have privatised their major airports. Some others are looking at private minority shareholdings or have established airports as separate, but still publicly-owned, corporations. In the USA, where one might expect privatisation to be attractive, it has not happened. For example, a proposal to privatise Albany Airport in New York State foundered mainly on the question of how to ensure that the airport continued to invest to meet demand rather than to maximise profits by raising prices and being cautious about new investment.

One of the reasons why there has not been more privatisation is probably that the scope for competition between airports - at least between airports serving major cities - is quite heavily constrained. I want to spend the next few minutes discussing why this is so.

The most obvious way in which airports can compete is for transfer traffic - that is, for those passengers who will need in any case to change aircraft or to travel via an intermediate point. If the intermediate airport is more attractive than its competitors in terms of convenience, efficiency, punctuality, lack of congestion, duty free facilities, etc., airlines will be able to develop a bigger network there than the airport would otherwise support. This form of competition is most evident in the United States where, for example, a passenger travelling from a medium-sized airport in California to another one in Florida may have the choice of Delta via Atlanta, American via Dallas, United via Denver, etc. At some airports the number of passengers making connections exceeds those beginning or ending their journeys there: Atlanta is the most frequently quoted example, but there are several others. Because particular airlines have focussed on, and indeed often dominate, particular hubs there is a close link between airline and airport competition.

In Europe, however, the proportion of connecting traffic is generally lower. There are several reasons for this. Historical factors, including restrictions on traffic rights, have no doubt played their part, but the main ones are probably geographical. A high proportion of journeys within Europe are short - both in terms of travel time and of length of stay - and this makes connecting flights unattractive where direct services are available. Thus the great majority of passengers in Europe are making single sector flights. Even at Heathrow, with its wide range of connections, over three-quarters of passengers begin or end their air journeys there. For these local passengers, choice of airport is mainly determined by closeness to their home or office and by the frequency of service on the route concerned relative to that offered from alternative airports. In the CAA we have done a lot of detailed work on what governs airport choice and what would be required to persuade people to use other airports. This work suggests that the preference which most people have for Heathrow over the other London airports is very strongly held, particularly by those passengers who pay the higher fares. It would take a very large increase in airport charges to price away Heathrow's excess demand. Given the economies of scale which large airports enjoy, smaller airports are in any case badly placed to compete on price. Even if they did, airport charges are only one component of airlines' total costs. Heathrow's charges can be as high as 8 per cent of total operating cost for a short domestic route in a small aircraft but they are a small fraction of the cost of operating a Boeing 747 to the USA. This means that on long or busy routes, to move a service from one airport to another simply to secure a reduction in airport charges at the London end would not be justified if it led to the loss of even one or two high-yield passengers per flight. Although Gatwick and Stansted have built up traffic in their own right, Stansted in particular will develop largely on the basis of overspill from Heathrow and subsequently from Gatwick. To a considerable extent the same is true of Luton.

At the time of privatisation some people suggested that the opportunity should be taken to split up BAA, or at least to sell one airport - possibly Gatwick - separately from the others. The Government decided not to do this. In its Airports Policy White Paper of 1985 it concluded that, while selling the airports separately would have reduced BAA's dominance, 'this option was found not to bring substantial real advantages, and to have important disadvantages'. However, this obviously means that BAA will continue to enjoy a near-monopoly of passengers who need to begin or end their journeys in the South East. It is for that reason that, in common with the other specialist regulators, we have a prominent and active rôle in price regulation. In particular, we are required to set the maximum levels of airport charges at Heathrow, Gatwick, Stansted and also at Manchester. I want to spend the rest of my time on a brief outline of our approach to this.

First, two important details. The regulated charges are only those for the landing, taking-off and parking of aircraft and for the handling of passengers through the terminals - about 40 per cent of the London airports' revenue. Yet we have to take into consideration all the airports' revenue - the so-called 'single-till' principle. This means that, on an RPI -X formula, relatively large changes in 'X' will have a relatively small impact on total revenue.

This raises an important question for later reviews. If revenue from other sources remains buoyant - and present indications are that it will - the single-till principle will continue to require further reductions in the proportion of total revenue which comes from the regulated charges. In theory these charges could not only fall below those costs specifically attributable to the airport charges activities, but they could become very low indeed or even negative. It would take several quinquennia to reduce the whole process to such absurdity, but I believe we will need to review it well before we get there. The details will not be easy. Airports are offering a genuine joint product in that the shops and offices would not survive without the core airport activities, and this gives rise to obvious problems of cost allocation. But I suspect the issue is much wider than the detail and we will have to reconsider the intrinsic logic of the single-till principle.

My second detailed point is this. Unlike the other newly privatised industries, where the regulator sets the price formula and the industry may in effect appeal to the MMC, the arrangements for airports work the other way round. We refer BAA's London airports and Manchester Airport to the MMC. The MMC advises us on the level of charges, but the final decision is ours. This rather complex process follows directly from the single-till principle. The MMC may make findings about the charges and costs of the activities which make up the other 60 per cent of BAA's income from its London airports. Any such findings must obviously be taken into account before the airport charges formula can be set. As a separate matter, if the MMC makes a public interest finding on the airports, as it did for example on the transparency of BAA's charging policy in certain areas, that is its decision and our rôle is simply to implement it.

Our basic approach to price regulation is similar to that adopted in the other industries. When we did our first review of the BAA formula last year (the first formula was set by the Secretary of State), we were quickly convinced that we should stay with the RPI -X approach. While the deficiencies of US-style rate of return regulation can be exaggerated, we believe it is important to establish the formula on the basis of a measure external to the company if efficiency incentives are to be maintained. Nevertheless, in setting 'X' the rate of return has to be the principal consideration. We know of no better criterion against which to judge whether users are paying a reasonable charge, and in any case the UK's international treaty obligations require us to focus on it. But we must also take into account other factors, of which the most important is future capacity needs, and here we were very much influenced on this by the views of the airlines which use the airports.

I will go into a little more detail on this point and raise what will by now be a familiar question. Our duty to encourage necessary investment in airport capacity, and the views of airlines on BAA's medium and long-term investment programme including Heathrow Terminal 5 and Heathrow Express, made it important to ensure that the formula was both fair to users in the period 1992-1997 and was consistent with BAA's need to attract capital to fund these projects. For this and other reasons we saw force in BAA's argument that, so far as possible, the value of 'X' in the later years of the new formula should reflect a reasonable expectation, insofar as one can judge it now, of what might be a sustainable value in the longer run. Discussion of the investment programme took us into the controversial area - which all the other regulators have also had to address - of the cost of capital. As you know, the experts use two methods of assessing this: the Capital Asset Pricing Model (CAPM) and the Dividend Growth Model (DGM) which attempt to estimate the cost of capital on the basic assumption of rational financial markets. The nature of this debate has been set out in several documents, including research papers, publications by regulators and, most recently, in a very helpful paper by Flemings Research. Flemings point out that the highly technical nature of the debate can draw one into thinking that the basic concepts are more scientific than in fact they are. Those of you who have read the report by MMC and by us on BAA will detect a similar scepticism. I am sure that we will have to revisit these issues in the next review.

I believe that the formula on which we finally settled - RPI-8 in the first two years, RPI-4 in the third year, and RPI-1 in the last two years - struck a reasonable balance between the need to ensure charges were fair and reasonable, the need to encourage necessary investment, and the need to create a stable framework for long-term planning. This formula means that BAA will receive some £100 million less over the quinquennium than would have been the case under the MMC's recommendations, and as part of this decision BAA committed itself to applying for planning permission for Terminal 5 at Heathrow. The healthy increase in the share price since the announcement of our decision suggests that the Stock Market at least did not regard it as a particularly harsh verdict.

We were, as I mentioned, influenced in the consultation phase by the views put to us by some of the airlines. But coming new to the process, I must confess that I was disappointed at the level of the debate. This is partly, I think, because so much of the information necessary to an informed discussion is suppressed on the grounds of commercial confidentiality. There is, of course, an economic model agreed between BAA, ourselves and the MMC indicating pre-tax profits, a return on capital employed, earnings per share, likely dividends per share, and so on, over the quinquennium on the basis of various pricing formulae. This is contained in the original MMC Report but most of it is taken out by the Secretary of State before publication, making it very difficult for other parties to put forward worthwhile views. It is by no means obvious that the publication of this information would be commercially damaging to a company such as BAA which has no direct competitors. The amount of information that can be made publicly available seems to me to be one of the more important issues affecting the regulation of a number of industries.

We are now embarked upon the quinquennial review for Manchester Airport. The MMC reported to us earlier this month. We will publish the MMC report and our own proposals early next month, seek people's views and make our final decision in the Autumn.

Conclusion

I hope I have been able to bring out why our regulatory rôle differs so markedly between the airline and the airport industries. In the airline industry we can rely quite heavily on market forces. Where we do intervene it is to deal with specific cases where they do not work effectively, although I have also raised some issues about the direction in which the industry appears to be going and the necessary part which a mergers and competition policy must play in maintaining a competitive industry.

In the case of airports, market forces are much less strong, and hence our much more forward rôle in price regulation where, as I have explained, we have to strike the balance between users' legitimate expectations that the prices will be no higher than necessary while ensuring that airports are able to carry out necessary investment and have continuing incentives to operate efficiently.

Clearly there are many unresolved issues for regulators and particular puzzles for regulators of monopolies. Having been responsible as a Minister for nationalised industries, I do know, however, that whatever the shortcomings of the existing system, the old one was worse. A Minister in such circumstances has to combine the rôles of regulator, Chairman of the holding company and principal banker - and he has to resolve the conflicts between the three behind closed doors. I welcome an evening such as this because it seems that, now that the rôles have been separated, it is very much in the public interest that the issues which divide regulators on the one hand from management, shareholders and bankers of the regulated industry on the other, should be open to scrutiny and debate.

AIRPORTS AND AIRLINE COMPETITION

DISCUSSANT:
Mr. Ian Jones
NERA

Introduction

MY TERMS OF REFERENCE are to identify and open up issues for discussion. Happily, this is not a difficult task on the present occasion. Chris Chataway has ranged widely over the issues that concern him as CAA chairman, at an exciting and eventful time for the civil aviation industry.

Airlines

It is appropriate, in a week which has seen the EC transport ministers agreeing a radical de-regulation package for European air services, that I should begin by considering the implications of this initiative.

An obvious starting point here is US experience, which suggests that in the long-run the EC package should bring substantial benefits to air travellers in general. However, there will also be losers, including those categories of customer who impose especially high costs on airlines through the need to provide on demand travel at peak times. One issue which we should consider is whether there is a case for some residual regulation to protect certain types of customer. I understand that the EC package contains a provision of this kind.

US experience also contains warnings for us. First, it clearly indicates the need for a vigorous and effective mergers policy at the EC level. Policy towards airline mergers in the US for much of the decade following de-regulation appears to have been based on the view that airline markets are contestable. Enough is now known about the competitive process in the de-regulated airline market to realise that whilst the industry may be workably competitive, it certainly does not satisfy the very strict requirements of a contestable market.

Although EC policy-makers will no doubt have learnt this lesson, it is still far from clear how effective EC merger policy is going to be in practice. There are two principal areas of concern here. One, which has been touched on by several commentators recently, including Sir Sydney Lipworth, is the problem of politicisation of decision-making. This is the fear that the fate of mergers may be decided not by reference to their impact on competition, but rather by appeal to woollier notions of industrial policy and the need to build community champions. The second and more technical point involves what appears to be a blind spot in the mergers regulation. The effect of this may be that the Commission is unable to block mergers which do not create or strengthen a dominant position, but which nevertheless lead to a significant increase in concentration. We may wish to return to this in discussion.

A second important lesson from the US is that the problem of market power in a de-regulated market is likely to be exacerbated by capacity shortages at key hub airports. This represents a very real entry barrier which could significantly impede the achievement of the potential benefits of de-regulation. Recent discussions have identified several options for public policy. First, there are the kind of administrative measures which the EC itself has proposed, involving the compulsory release of slots by incumbent airlines. Second, there is the possibility of auctioning slots. Third, more realistic posted prices might be set for airport slots, combined with the possibility of trading in slots. The relative merits of these three approaches is certainly an issue to take up in discussion. To start the ball rolling, I would suggest that anything like a full-scale auction approach is simply not feasible, because of complexities introduced by demand complementarities. If this approach is not feasible, then I would prefer to rely on posted prices rather than administrative processes.

Airports

Chris Chataway has referred to the resetting of BAA's price cap. I personally took a close interest in this process, having worked as a member of the NERA team whose recommendations formed the basis for BAA's current price cap régime.

NERA's report to the Department of Transport concluded on an optimistic note: economic regulation by means of price control based on these considerations would encourage the more efficient running of BAA's airports; would ensure that benefits of improved efficiency and commercial performance would be shared between BAA's customers and BAA; would be comprehensible to investors; would be administratively workable; would encourage appropriate investment at airports in new facilities; and would be compatible with the UK's international obligations.

How have things worked out in practice? I think quite honestly that it is too soon to tell. I would suggest that, in common with other privatised utilities, BAA was given a relatively easy ride with its initial (RPI -1) price cap. In particular, I believe that under a more demanding régime, the company would have taken a tighter grip of its labour costs than appears to have been the case from the evidence presented in the MMC report.

As Chris Chataway noted, the BAA price formula review process is distinctive in giving the MMC 'first innings'. The process has certain merits in terms of the public interest. It generates much fuller information in the public domain about the conduct and performance of the regulated than is available in other industries. For BAA, the MMC has produced what amounts to a 300-page costs and efficiency report on the company. Notwithstanding the many deletions in the report, most of them quite trivial, this compares very favourably with the quite meagre information which has emerged on company performance from other price formula reviews.

The relatively open nature of the process also requires the regulatory agencies involved to be more careful and explicit in justifying their conclusions than if everything is settled in negotiation. The long and carefully argued reports prepared by both the Commission and the CAA again compare very favourably with the somewhat terse and cloudy statements which have emanated from Oftel and Ofgas recently. I wonder if other people share my perceptions of the relative merits of the two types of regulatory process?

I turn finally to an issue which Chris Chataway has alluded to and which has arisen in the ongoing arbitration with the US government over airport charges at Heathrow. Do airports offer a joint product, as Chris has suggested, and as was argued by the American side in the arbitration, and, if so, what are the implications for pricing airport services?

If the services provided by airports are in strict joint demand, as are the demands for left- and right-foot shoes, then the total cost of producing the set of airport services should be most efficiently recovered from the individual services on the basis of demand intensities. The fact is, though, that airport services are not jointly demanded. Some travellers who fly in and out of Heathrow use the airport parking facilities; some do not. Some patronise duty free shops and restaurants, others do not. Aircraft come in different shapes and sizes and make use of airside facilities in different proportions. And so on. As argued by UK government witnesses at the arbitration, such a situation requires that both commercial and aviation services should be priced separately to reflect their respective marginal costs.

This clearly is not happening at the moment. Aviation services at Heathrow are being priced far below marginal costs; commercial services generally far above. Unfortunately, the problem is exacerbated by the existing price cap régime, which only restricts aviation charges. Rather than revisiting the single-till principle, as Chris Chataway suggests, I believe that in the long run a more appropriate remedy may be, first, to restrict or abolish the fiscal privileges currently enjoyed by airports, and, second, to bring the full range of airport outputs into the scope of the price control formula. On that possibly controversial note, I will hand the discussion back to the Chairman.